African Belief and Knowledge Systems: A Critical Perspective

Munyaradzi Mawere

Langaa Research & Publishing CIG
Mankon, Bamenda

Publisher
Langaa RPCIG
Langaa Research & Publishing Common Initiative Group
P.O. Box 902 Mankon
Bamenda
North West Region
Cameroon
Langaagrp@gmail.com
www.langaa-rpcig.net

Distributed in and outside N. America by African Books Collective
orders@africanbookscollective.com
www.africanbookcollective.com

ISBN: 9956-726-85-0

© Munyaradzi Mawere 2011

DISCLAIMER
All views expressed in this publication are those of the author and do not necessarily reflect the views of Langaa RPCIG.

Dedication

To my late mom and dad, Sarah and Enock Mawere, I humbly, gratefully and posthumously dedicate this book, which you initiated but never lived long enough to behold its blossoming.

Table of Contents

Preface.. v
Introduction... ix

Chapter One.. 1
Defining Metaphysics... 1
The Sad History of Metaphysics... 4
Earlier Positivism... 6
Metaphysics Rejected... 9
The Indispensability of Metaphysics....................................... 10
Metaphysics a Winner?: A Critical Appraisal......................... 12

Chapter Two.. 17
Uncovering African Metaphysics.. 17
African Metaphysics' Struggle for Recognition..................... 21
Beneath African Traditional Culture....................................... 25
The Continued Relevance of African Metaphysics................. 28
The Compatibility of African and Western Metaphysics........ 30

Chapter Three... 37
Ontology and Concepts in African Metaphysics.................... 37
The Concept of Being African Metaphysics........................... 38
The Conception of Person in African Metaphysics................ 41
Causality and the Two Worlds of Africa................................ 46
The Conception of Time in African Metaphysical Discourse....... 49

Chapter Four... 57
The Nexus between African metaphysics and Indigenous Epistemologies.. 57
Indigenous Knowledge System as African Epistemology........... 59
African Epistemology and the Fallacy of Science.................. 61
The Persisting Link between African Epistemology and African Metaphysics.. 65

iii

Chapter Five... 77
African Indigenous Epistemologies.. 77
Taboos as African Epistemology System...................................... 81
The Metaphysics and Epistemology of *Ngozi*........................... 85
Epistemologies Enshrouded in *Runyoka* and *Rukwa*................ 87
Witchcraft as Indigenous Metaphysical Epistemology................ 90

Chapter Six.. 105
African Indigenous Ways of Knowing... 105
Categorizing African Ways of Knowing...................................... 106
The Supernatural Way of Knowing... 106
Divination.. 106
Revelation and Faith.. 108
The Natural Way... 109
Paranormal.. 111
On Behalf of African Metaphysical Epistemology...................... 113

Preface

While acknowledging the contribution of western knowledge systems to the development of modern Africa and harbouring no wishes to turn back the clock of development to the past, this book focuses on how African metaphysics and African epistemology heretofore referred to as African metaphysical epistemology has suffered dislocations, distortions and pejorative labels until recent times. African metaphysical epistemology is a collection of concepts, practices, patterns, symbols, and terms from various African cultures, past and present, continental and in the African Diaspora as a resource for discussing 21st century perceptions of the person, time and phenomena[1]. In the light of this observation, I register my desire to restore, reconstruct and reaffirm African heritage, culture and identity by way of advocating for metaphysical epistemology to have a place in college and university curricula. I believe the fruits of this effort will be a blessing; not just to Africa, but also to the world, which benefits immensely from the increasing availability of the treasure of African spirituality and religious culture rendered metaphysically and epistemologically and in ways conforming to the discursive parameters of scholarly works.

    I have chosen to discuss African metaphysics and African epistemology together not only because they are closely tied together, but because the two are the wellsprings of African philosophy in general and have suffered in many ways similar; hence their treatment in unison as African metaphysical epistemology. Both need restoration and reconstruction. The main problem, however, still have to do with whether we can in any meaningful and coherent manner talk about an African metaphysical epistemology that covers or incorporates the inevitable nuances that go with cultural and individual differences of the African people in the continent and those in the Diaspora. I have adopted the principles of charity where in hermeneutical studies I am allowed to carry out my interpretation with some sense of liberalism and assumption which is not harmful to the spirit of interpretation and writing. As such, I have assumed that all Africans in the continent and those in Diaspora are bound to have more in common than with people of other continents. Also, I have not pretended to say everything in African metaphysics and African epistemology in this book. I have used more examples from some African countries than others, but making sure not to lose focus in my treatment of metaphysical epistemology in Africa as a whole.

For a majority of students of philosophy, African cultural studies and Social anthropology, this is a text they would enjoy reading. It quests to show them the wisdom that lies in traditional African metaphysical epistemology and encourage them to start on the path of critical thinking for themselves. The book, above all else, attempts to show that questioning and indeed right questioning matters most, not only in philosophy but other spheres of life. I have attempted to unravel and explicate the epistemological basis of African metaphysical epistemology which has to do with "being" and its ontological appurtenances like personality, substance, essence, *force vitale*, among others, and to see how these differ from western conceptions.

Using concepts pervasive in African culture and western metaphysics like "being", "time" and others, I have also examined how African metaphysical epistemology includes and transcends the western explanatory indices and epistemological bodies. While the westerners limit their inquiry to experience and reason, Africans go beyond that to employ extra empirical and extra-ratiocinative means often called extra-sensory perception and or mystic ways of knowing. The latter point makes the adhesive bond between African metaphysics and African epistemology even stronger – it also justifies the treatment of both in the same volume as the present.

I acknowledged that one of the most vibrant subject of debate among African and non-African scholars in the 20th and 21st centuries centred on the existence of African philosophy. Yet, much of these early works especially by African scholars struggled to radiate sufficient light to break free and liberate African philosophies (like African metaphysics and African epistemology) from the long and heavy shadows of colonialism and cultural imperialism. I should not be mistaken to be arguing for a going back to discussions or debates on the existence of African philosophy. Instead, I submit that this debate is no longer necessary in the present era. What is necessary now is urgency; to move beyond the question of African philosophy's existence debate. If African philosophy exists, African philosophers should show it, practice it and put it on paper rather than continue talking about it or engaging in endless talks about it. What this book does more than any other anthology on African philosophy, African cultural studies and Social anthropology on Africa is to show and model the metaphysical and epistemological lances, reasoning processes and "indigenous" methodologies of Africa. It provides an accessible, thought provocative metaphysical and epistemological issues that are solidly grounded on Africa.

More important has been my fervent hope to produce a text that would be hospitable to instructors and students of differing persuasions and that would allow the former to develop the course as they desire. This hope is reflected in two ways in this book: First, I try to keep most of my own leanings in the background as much as possible, although it is doubtless inevitable that my choice of topics and the presentation of the material reflect some of my sympathies. Second, I make no attempt to resolve or settle the major issues for the readers, but rather provide them with the resources to come to their own understanding of the direction they should take. In any case, the text can be used in a class of metaphysics, epistemology, ecology, African studies, cultural studies, social anthropology, and, of course, in courses that bridge metaphysics and epistemology-what I call here 'metaphysical epistemology'.

Notes

1. Denise Martin, Pan African Metaphysical Epistemology: A Pentagonal Introduction, *Journal of Pan African Studies*, 2008:.2(.3).

Introduction

This is a book about African metaphysical epistemology. It is intended for both students and anyone else who is interested in the subject. Although I examine metaphysics and epistemology in general, I am more concerned about the interface of African metaphysics and African epistemology and how these can be recognized as legitimate disciplines in college and university curricula. The teaching of such disciplines would create space for co-creation and a shared as well as balanced globalization in the production and advancement of knowledge.

It is common for an introductory text as this to begin with a general characterization of its study. It seems obvious that to understand what African metaphysical epistemology is we have to understand something of both metaphysics and epistemology. While most of us have more or less some idea of the history of Africa as a continent, few of us have any clear idea at all of what Africa's metaphysical epistemology is.

The subject of African metaphysical epistemology is a very broad and far reaching inquiry. In any case, there are some strategic hurdles to overcome. The first is the connection between African metaphysics and African "indigenous" knowledge systems heretofore referred to as African epistemology. Is it possible to connect the two and still make sense in the debate about African metaphysics and African epistemology at one hand, and the debate about African metaphysical epistemology on the other hand? The second problem pertains to the geographical epithet "Africa". Is it possible to develop a broad outline or rather a complete view of metaphysical epistemology from the perspective of a geographical area, a continent – Africa – which is only a part of the world? Wouldn't the context of such a perspective fly into the face of the assumed universality of the ideas of metaphysics and epistemology, going against the grain of its inter-subjective and therefore international use? Or wouldn't this tantamount to lapsing into a kind of truncated conception of metaphysical epistemology, leaving us with nothing but the narrow vision of local biases, interests and viewpoints? Furthermore, would such a perspective, if it can be circumscribed at all, do justice to a wide range of the metaphysical and epistemological experiences of millions of people of Africa who themselves have different cultural histories and circumstances? Perhaps the consoling goad to all these questions is the fact that no work can claim to say all that need be said on any subject matter. What is important in any given work is to have a clear vision of what is intended to be achieved. This is not to say that the questions above shall not be fully addressed and examined in this text. In fact, I would like to contend that these questions can be addressed and objections arise overcome if one takes as a starting point that metaphysical and epistemological issues in Africa, as they are the world over, can never be divorced from people's issues, cultural issues and rational issues. At the same time I would like to draw attention to the fact that general theories, should be related to, if not evaluated from the view point of certain key experiences and questions of people in a particular geographical setting and circumstances. I feel, therefore, persuaded that these hurdles can be safely handled and overcome in this book.

Much has been said on different aspects of metaphysics and epistemology in general. However, it should be noted that western metaphysics and epistemology are basically a history of individual metaphysicians and epistemologists whose ideas have been written and preserved on paper. Contrary-wise, African metaphysics and African epistemology do not belong to individual people. The two (African metaphysics and African epistemology) are largely integrated within the African traditional cultures. And it is even difficult to talk of African metaphysics without mentioning African epistemology (or vice versa) and of course culture. For this reason, nothing much on African metaphysics and African epistemology in particular has been documented. Even with the recent publications by prominent African philosophers on African philosophy like John Mbiti, Paulin Hountondji, Tsenay Serequeban Odera Oruka, among a few others, no written texts especially focusing on African metaphysics and African epistemology in particular have been developed so far; what has been written are works that are mostly dependent on orally transmitted ideas and works that claim to represent African philosophy in general. This in itself leads curious readers to question whether there are no branches of philosophy that can be identified and talked of as is with the case of western philosophy. One thus can raise a crucial question: If western philosophy has branches such as Metaphysics, Epistemology, Logic, and Ethics/Moral philosophy, Aesthetics and others, why not African philosophy? Can't we have philosophy branches as African metaphysics and African epistemology studied in colleges and universities? It is precisely this area fusing irenicism and intellectual courage that shines through the pages of this book. I seek to fill in gaps in history to link the past to the present, and speak for the adaptation of African philosophies in higher academic institutions. For this to happen, a study of the cultures, particularly the "cultural ideals" is necessary to bring to light what may be considered the main indices of the African traditional metaphysical and epistemological systems of thought. In other words, culture reflects the people's attitude towards life and the world they live in; it determines what the people consider as fundamental and promotive of their sense of the meaning of human existence.

As been previously highlighted, otherwise though implicitly, Africans have a very old but rich philosophy, much of which is unrecorded. Besides evidence from proverbs, riddles, idioms and folklore among other literary genres, not much has been done in terms of scholarship to support Africa's enduring metaphysical and epistemological views. There is literary poverty on Africa, especially by African scholars on these specific areas. It is the motivation of this work to bring to record African metaphysical epistemology and demonstrate how this can complement western "packages of knowledge" and help the world attaining a deeper and holistic understanding of reality. Also, these philosophies – African epistemology and African metaphysics – should not be left to fall out of use in theory and practice since they are valuable archives of the history, identity and culture of various ethnic communities in Africa. Western literature seems to have often failed to recognize the significance of local literature and the role it plays in describing, defining, identifying and relating Africans to their social and physical environment. It is only through post-colonial discourses such as one adumbrated in this book that a shift to a more Afro-centric perspective that shows more interest in local cultures, philosophies and literature can be promoted.

Reinforcing my argument above, I take my readers to the reality that African metaphysics as is the case with African epistemology is still at an infant stage as philosophical disciplines even in African universities. Even African scholars themselves seem to preach what they don't do-call for recognition of African philosophy which they don't teach in their universities. Part of the reason is that these philosophies like African philosophy itself have suffered a false and pernicious consciousness that has been nurtured over the centuries by some western influential philosophers - David Hume, George W.F. Hegel, Immanuel Kant, Lucien Levy-Bruhl and Diedrich Westermann – philosophers who describe Africans as a *tabula rasa* – a people with no reason/rationality; hence without a philosophy and worse still a metaphysical or epistemological theory. These western scholars have unsympathetically labelled Africa a dark continent[1] – a false and pejorative label that has even served as the rationale for slavery, colonialism, discrimination and other forms of Euro-centrism and domination. Mindful of this fact, the metaphysical and epistemological stances of this book are critical. Like Critical paradigm's purpose, the book seeks to overcome modes of social, psychological domination and oppression. The Critical approach to emancipation espouses that:

A society owes emancipation from the external forces of nature to labour processes, that is, to the production of technically exploitable knowledge [...]. Emancipation from the compulsion of internal nature succeeds to the degree that institutions based on force are replaced by an organization of social relations that are bound only to communication free from domination[2].

I infer from Habermas that emancipation of African scholars from hegemonic practices emerges from scientific knowledge production, self-reflection and social relations based on democratic communication.

Yet it is not only Africa that has suffered threats from some scholars, but western metaphysics itself. The latter has suffered serious threats from scientism, particularly the verification criterion of the logical positivists of the 1920s. Logical positivism (a doctrine postulated by logical positivists) asserts that philosophy should be restricted to the clarification and explanation of scientific theorizing[3]. The logical positivists attempt to achieve two interrelated things: firstly the subordination of philosophy to science and secondly the exclusion of metaphysics represented by any attempt to go beyond what is given in experience or what Hume would prefer to call "matters of facts"[4]. The positivists hoped to realize this goal through their famous "Verifiability Principle" which is taken to mean that the meaning of a proposition consists in its method of verification. Thus, as can be seen, the threats by scientism targeted not only Western metaphysics, but also African metaphysics and mystical ways of knowing – indigenous epistemologies.

I cannot pretend to identify and articulate, in this book, all what we call African metaphysical epistemology. What I attempt therefore to do is to carry out some intellectual examination of the essential elements of what is conventionally conceived as African metaphysical epistemology. As a first text of its own kind, I have decided to discuss African metaphysics and African epistemology together. And the name I have attributed to the duo is African metaphysical epistemology, a concept that is commonly used by most contemporary African scholars who research on African culture and philosophies. This conception is the emergent basis of the debate on African philosophy and of course, African metaphysics and epistemology in particular. Though this book does not focus on African philosophy but African metaphysics and epistemology, defining the focus of my work will allay the fears of prominent African philosophers mentioned above whom are bound to smell a rat any time attempt is made to talk of African philosophy as a static, collective and ideological set of beliefs which lie in the immutable sail of the African people.

It should be remarked that the birth of the debate on African philosophy is historically associated with two related events namely: Western discourse on Africa, and the African response to it. At the centre of this debate is the concept of reason, a value which is believed to stand as the great divide between the civilized and the uncivilized, the logical and the mystical[5], the scientific and non-scientific. This observation concurs with many African scholars who believe that African ideological definition of philosophy is what is normally called to use when examining African philosophy in general, culture and people. This leads to the conception of African philosophy as a kind of wisdom, individual or collective, a set of principles presenting some decree of coherence and intended to govern the daily practice of a man or people of Africa.

In this book, I go beyond this conception to pointing out that cultural philosophy born out African philosophy like African metaphysics and African epistemology must have certain underlying logic to explain its complexities. However, it will be a mark of intellectual philistinism to continue to hold that all Africans conceive reality woof and weft from exactly the same perspective. What Africans have are similar out-looks and spiritual inspiration which enjoy a higher semblance than with views outside the African context. The object of this book is to look at the drawing board and see how one can stand with the spate or write-ups on African metaphysics and African epistemology heretofore referred to as African metaphysical epistemology.

For purposes of thoroughness in my discussion, the first chapter of this book focuses on metaphysics in general. The second and third chapters discuss African metaphysics. Chapters four and five examine African epistemology and its nexus with the twin sister discipline of African metaphysics. And the last chapter looks at African ways of knowing. The arrangement of chapters, as they are, will enable me to count my successes and failures as I continue in this philosophical journey of reconstructing African metaphysical epistemology. This intellectual inventory will enable me to up-date, redirect and fill in the "African gap" that for a long time has been left wide open. It is indeed, more than its predecessors, a representation of the celebration of African culture as well as a demonstration of African philosophers' commitment to reform Philosophy's curriculum and exhibit a broad outline of African metaphysics and African epistemology that can be taught as independent courses in Universities and Colleges the world-over. This is necessary because the implications of African metaphysical epistemology in higher education are critical especially to African students and those who study Africa. They are more likely to utilize student development models which are culturally relevant, thereby more useful to them. I should be quick, however, to note that African metaphysical epistemology might be important, but not necessarily as a universal application for all students but as an alternative to the predominant European metaphysics and epistemology, which does not fully accommodate the historical development of African students.

Notes

1. For more details on Hume, Hegel, Kant, Levy-Bruhl and Westermann about their view of Africa see Winch, pp. 1970, "Understanding a primitive society" in B. Wilson (Ed.), Rationality, Oxford: Basil Blackwell, pp. 79; Churchland, P.M. 1984, Matter and Consciousness, Cambridge, The MIT Press, p.73 or Ramose, M.B. 1999, African philosophy through Ubuntu, Harare: Mond Books, pp.44.

2. Habermas, J. *Knowledge and human interests.* London: Heinemann, 1972, pp.53.

3. "Logical positivism" in Richard A. Popkin (Ed.) 1999.The Columbia History of Western Philosophy. New York: Columbia University Press, pp.621.

4. Ayer. A. J. the Vienna circle in Midwest Studies in Philosophy. Vol. VI, 1981, pp. 183.

5. Masolo, D.A. African Philosophy in Search of Identity, Nairobi: East African Educational Publishers, 1995.

Chapter One

Defining Metaphysics

It is unwise to delve into the subject of African metaphysical epistemology before defining metaphysics. It is therefore necessary to first of all pay some attention to the subject metaphysics itself.

The word "metaphysics" is believed to have been first used in the 4th century BC by the peripatetic. Its etymological definition holds that the term derived from the Greek words meta-ta-physika meaning "after physics"[1] or transcending the physical as metaphysics is concerned with issues bordering on the extra-mental, spiritual, abstract, universal or the transcendental. Among philosophers, from Descartes onwards, the term metaphysics has come to have the distinct sense of having to do with what lies beyond what is available to the senses -the physics- with what is not merely abstract but in some sense transcendent as well[2]. Metaphysics thus has become an attempt to arrive by rational means at a rational picture of the world. Following from the above, metaphysics can be generally understood as a core branch of philosophical discourse which focuses on the fundamental question of the ultimate nature of things and scope of reality in its totality. Unlike natural sciences such as mathematics, physics and chemistry, metaphysics raises ontological and critical questions that have to do with the "whatness" and "whyness" of all things in the realm of existence. This means that the term metaphysics can be a bit confusing and intimidating as unlike other disciplines such as biology or geography which start with a clear definition of the subject to be studied, the subject of metaphysics like philosophy itself is difficult to offer such a clear definition. Consequently, different people tended to offer different answers. Michael Loux's in his Universals and Particulars: Readings and Ontology, for example, captures the different areas of concern of metaphysics, which include ontology. Yet, for Martin Heidegger, all ontological inquiries have missed the mark by not addressing satisfactorily the question of being. Realizing the complexity of dealing with metaphysical issues, a contemporary philosopher, Anthony O'Hear, rightly defines metaphysics as the study of what

1

there is[3]-the ultimate/complete reality of all things in the realm of existence-material or immaterial. O'Hear goes beyond Heidegger in stressing that the condition of "being" or existence which is central to metaphysics is holistic and hence seeks to answer two questions: 1) ontology (existence of all things- material and immaterial) and 2) predication (what can be said about existing things/entities). Owing to the complexities of metaphysics, all issues that seem incomprehensible by common sense or unverifiable by expert science such as spiritual entities traditionally fall in the realm of metaphysics.

Though metaphysics has variously been defined, for example, as the science of the ultimate or super-sensible reality, it enjoys a more strict definition as the science of being qua being. The history of philosophy from its inception has been the history of attempts at determining what this being qua being as the ultimate reality is all about. Historically, Parmenides is often referred to as the real enunciator of western metaphysics before Socrates, Plato and Aristotle gave it a more detailed and rigorous treatment as a wholesome discipline. Down to Immanuel Kant and further to the present, metaphysics became divided into three major parts, namely: rational theology, rational cosmology and rational psychology. Kant, thus sees Metaphysics as concerning the totality of reality whether God as in rational theology; or man, nature and the universe as in rational cosmology or mind and its ideas as in rational psychology. However, these are not periscope wholly through a priori concepts or a posteriori concepts alone as rationalists and empiricist philosophers respectively, have argued but through the interplay of a priori and a posteriori concepts or through experience and reason. This understanding still agrees with great philosophers as Descartes who (though a rationalist) has come to understand metaphysics as a philosophy discipline to do with what lies beyond what is available to the senses, and not what is merely abstract but in some sense transcendent as well[4]. Thus metaphysicians generally agree, though in different semantics, that metaphysics is a science that seeks ultimate understanding of reality of all things in the realm of existence.

It is worth noting, however, that historically, the word metaphysics has been speculated to have entered the philosophical lexicon when part of a group of Aristotle's treaties which himself called "first philosophy," now called his metaphysics, were found untitled by an early Editor and Chronicler of Aristotle's work on physical nature, Andronicus (of 1st century AD), but after the work entitled Physics. Aristotle refers to this untitled work "the science of being qua being"[5] which meant it was seen as the science of being equal being. Its aim was to investigate the general nature of ultimate being/reality/existence. This means metaphysics' aim has always to study reality from the point of view of other beings. Since then the word metaphysics has been used to denote reality transcending the world of science and common sense. As such, metaphysics is believed to be one of the most difficult branches of philosophy. This complexity of metaphysics as a discipline has been alluded to by various scholars. Bruce Aune, for example, philosophizes that metaphysics is possibly the most basic but certainly the most controversial and difficult part of philosophy[6]. In a previous research, Jancar had acknowledged that though the most important of all Aristotle's works, metaphysics is the most difficult of Aristotle's books. As such, a great Arabian philosopher of the 11th A.D Century, Avicenna (980-1037) is said to have read the work forty times without understanding a word[7]. The complexity is chiefly because of metaphysics being a subject that includes both transcends and particulars of individual existence and penetrates the interrelationships of particulars within the universal. In this sense, metaphysics can be understood as a philosophical outlook which tries to reach a more comprehensive, all-embracing, wholesome, totalistic view of the reality of "beings" without neglecting the unique place of individual "beings" in the holism of reality. Here, by reality I mean both disparate and homogenous outlooks of things. Metaphysics thus may be an aspect of reality such as properties, relations, individual beings meant to understand the whole in its totality- it could be the examination of "being" in a generic sense. What is important in each case is to reach general and fundamental assumption that articulate a rationally acceptable world view as far as such sphere of reality is concerned.

  Underscoring the discussion above, one would note that metaphysics deals with the nature and scope of existence in its totality. Being the study of reality as a whole, metaphysics is concerned with the generalization of experience for the purpose of identifying fundamental entities, both in material and immaterial forms. Metaphysics therefore involves a synthesis of all experiences in order to achieve a coherent whole, which gives a complete picture of reality. Yet, from time to time in the history of philosophical thought scientists and philosophers of a positivist tendency have produced a criterion of meaningfulness with which metaphysics was judged nonsense. We turn now to a discussion on the sad history of metaphysics before making a case for metaphysics.

The Sad History of Metaphysics

Metaphysics has a reputation, not entirely undeserved, for concentrating on abstruse and difficult questions which, as critics charge, are far removed from commonplace things, our day to day life and the immediate world in which we live. Metaphysical thought thus is believed by many critics, especially those from a natural science orientation, as a body of mere beliefs and not a tool of exploration. This identification of metaphysics as a body of mere beliefs and not as a fundamental science or tool of exploration has incidentally been the root of most harsh and destructive criticisms against metaphysics as a quest in futility.

Metaphysics, thus, has been susceptible to attacks by natural scientists and most harshly by the so-called "logical positivists" with their doctrine "logical positivism". Although, the exact date when logical positivism began may not be easily ascertained, according to records, it started in the early 1920s following a confluence of philosopher scientists, physicists, mathematicians and psychologists proclaiming themselves logical positivists or Vienna circle movement whose intention was to rub minds and discuss issues of common interests. The initial or founding members were few but as the movement grew in fame and popularity, it attracted a wider membership particularly from England, Holland, Belgium, America, Australia and Germany. The founding members included Moritz Schlick (1882-1945), (who incidentally occupied the Professorial Chair vacated by Ernst Mach). Rudolf Carnap (1891- 1970), Otto Neurath (1882- 1945), Herbert Feigl (1902-1973), Friedrick

Waismann (1896-1960), Kurt Geodel (1906-1978), and A. J. Ayer (1910-1989). Even though Ayer was a late comer to the circle, he eventually became its anchorman and most popular spokesman. There is confusion as to whether Wittgenstein was also a logical positivist or not. I will clear this confusion here and now. Wittgenstein cannot be said to be a member of the Circle in the truest sense of the word since he never officially subscribed to it. However, he lived nearby in Vienna and maintained constant dialogue with Schlick and Waismann.

It is most important to remark that when the Circle was formulated and made public its philosophical orientation, the publication of Wittgenstein's Tractatus Logico-Philosophicus in 1921 and Ayer's Language, Truth and Logic in 1936 boosted the image and reinforced the ideas already articulated in the Circle's journal Erkenntnis, which had since served as a formidable outlet for the dissemination of its views, and adding a substantial impetus to its growth[8]. Having made this remark, a critical question now is: "What were the views of the logical positivists and what were they for and against?"

The position of the logical positivists can be derived from their expressed aim which is to show that all genuine knowledge are those related to logic, mathematics, and the natural sciences. In other words, they argue that the only genuine knowledge is knowledge about the physical world and the only means of attaining such knowledge is science. Based on this ideology, one expects that there is no place for such conceptualizations which border on metaphysical knowledge of reality or supra-natural or theoretical entities which transcend what is permissible in common-sense experience. Following from this, one notices that the logical positivists attempt to achieve two interrelated things, firstly, the subordination of philosophy to science and secondly the exclusion of metaphysics and its inquiries represented by any attempt to go beyond what is given in experience or what Hume would prefer to call "matters of fact"[9]. The logical positivists hoped to realize this goal through their famous "Principle of Verification" which is taken to mean that the meaning of a proposition consists in its method of verification. The strategy, according to them, is that if one, for example, wants to verify the proposition: "The professor is in the lecture room," it is expected that the person who uttered the statement actually sees the professor in the lecture room and that the person knows the meaning of the proposition "the professor is in the lecture room" as well as its rendering; otherwise the proposition would be considered empty and meaningless.

It is curious to note that the stance held by the logical positivists in their attempt to do away with metaphysics was not new at all. Earlier attempts had been made by empiricist philosophers, John Locke, David Hume, and also Comte among others; hence we shall briefly look at earlier positivism in the next section.

Earlier Positivism

With the verification criterion the logical positivists were fascinated by the empirical and scientific tempers of the day. As said earlier on in section 1.1, logical positivism is a radical form of scientism started in the 1920s holding that only the special sciences can make cognitively meaningful statements about the world. It rejects traditional philosophy especially metaphysics as it requires that philosophy should be restricted to the clarification and explanation of scientific theorizing[10]. Yet, the attempt of logical positivism's (though was not called by the same name) to interpret and render futile traditional philosophy on the empiricist and scientific moorings was earlier elaborated by the 17th century empiricists philosophers, John Locke and David Hume. The duo argued that an observation consists in having a particular sense experience, a particular datum with which one is directly acquainted devoid of mistakes or errors. Also Hume classified propositions into two, namely formal and factual propositions while Locke relates to logic and mathematics whose truth is tautologous since its truth is known by a mere analysis of the meaning of the propositions[11]. We have just introduced the term proposition and that must be explained before we go on. A proposition can be characterized as whatever can be either true or false[12]. Consider the sentence: "It will rain in the afternoon". This can be authenticated (if it does rain in the afternoon) or falsified (if it fails to rain in the afternoon). Consider yet another example of a proposition: "All spinsters are unmarried" whose truth is immediately known if we know the meaning of the word spinster. This proposition is said to be analytic, necessary, or a priori as it is known merely on the basis of rationally. And some propositions like "All cubes have six sides," and "All men are mortal" require empirical verification to ascertain their truth or falsity since it is not part of the definition of "cube" and "man" respectively that they are six-sided and mortal respectively, but only that, past experience and observation has shown that cubes are six sided and that men do die at a certain age. Propositions such as these are said to be synthetic, empirical, contingent or a posteriori. This is what Hume would call factual propositions. Locke and Hume, the two earlier logical positivists as I shall call them (though were not called by this name), accepted this classification and that of Auguste Comte's (1798-1857) "law of three stages" in which he said all knowledge and societies dialectically pass through theological and metaphysical stages before they come to be recognized as positive or scientific societies[13]. Comte rejected the theological and metaphysical stages to be considered scientific because thought or conceptualizations here are suffused with myths, fictions and gods. But in the positive or scientific stage explanation of phenomena is done through its connections to some general laws, like the gravitational law.

Generally speaking, modern science which took shape during the 17th-century's scientific revolution, culminating with Isaac Newton's Mathematical Principles of Natural Philosophy of 1687, was a fatal blow to religion and philosophy in general. It stressed two major conditions:

1) It demanded that a scientific theory be empirically testable and;

2) That a theory be able to explain particular phenomena and should have its laws or principles stated in terms of mathematical relations between features of the world that could be measured and quantified-calculated.

It is clear that no reference to God and religion can enter into any mathematical formulae that are the expressions of laws of physical science. The same applies to all metaphysical pursuits. Though this recognition did not, however, entail that scientists must give up religion and metaphysicians give up metaphysical inquiries the general atmosphere was inclined towards science and the abandonment of all that cannot be empirically verified or quantified.

In view of this I underscore the argument that, besides Locke and Hume's empiricism, Isaac Newton, Bertrand Russell, G. E. Moore, Wittgenstein among others who championed the analytic movement which regards philosophy as essentially concerned with logical analysis, logical synthesis and comprehensive construction of facts as they exist in the world were also among the school of earlier logical positivism. All these scholars reacted, though to varying degrees, to G. W. F Hegel's (1770-1830) metaphysical idealism. It should be recalled that before the emergence of the analytic movement, philosophy seemed to be dominated by the metaphysical idealism of Hegel which was popularized by both Bradley and McTaggart who said that the "absolute" is a community of substances which is seen as part of the whole. The analytic philosophy thus arose as a revolt against this metaphysical idealism and to reconstruct philosophy along the paradigmatic framework of science, mathematics and logic. This bold step dovetailed in logical atomism which was defended by Russell and Wittgenstein. Though Wittgenstein did not officially subscribe to logical positivism, he nevertheless maintained personal interactions with some of the Circle's members. Again, his book, Tractatus added an impetus as well as reinforcing the Circle's views. For in the Tractatus, Wittgenstein has it that "propositions comprise of atomic facts which are logically independent of each other"[14]. Following his explanation, these atomic or basic facts are mirrored by elementary propositions. In order to determine whether a proposition is cognitively significant, such proposition, must be capable of being expressed either as true or false. Put differently, a proposition is said to be cognitively meaningful in so far as it matches or corresponds to the states of affairs in the world, such as the proposition, "The professor is in the lecture room" whose cognitive sense can be comprehended within what is empirically observable like "professor" and "lecture room" in the world. Hence, in the Tractatus, he stated that "what we cannot speak about we must pass over in silence," although, he seemed to equivocate at the end of the book when he said that "all those who understood him would understand that everything he had said was nonsense." This alone was enough to label Wittgenstein as one scholar among those who earlier before the 1920s logical positivists had already set a strong case against metaphysics.

A corollary to Wittgenstein is Ayer's powerful book, Language. Truth and Logic which, like Tractatus, expresses the view that genuine philosophical problems can be solved by logical analysis and that all propositions are susceptible to either "practical verification" or "verification in principle". Metaphysical propositions judged against this principle could not pass the test. These efforts by earlier scholars such as Locke, Hume, Comte, Russell, Wittgenstein and the 1920s logical positivists were not just empty threats to metaphysics. They indeed brought fatal consequences to metaphysics as a discipline. In the next few pages we will examine these consequences.

Metaphysics Rejected

From the works of Locke, Hume, Comte and Wittgenstein among others, the logical positivists attempted to determine the status of religious, metaphysical, ethical and poetical statements using their verification criteria. They sought to examine whether or not they would pass the test of empirical verifications which expectedly they failed to satisfy. According to them, since such propositions of philosophical literature, religion/ theology, arts, metaphysics and ethics bear emotive meaning; they do not satisfy the empirical verification principle. As such, all such propositions are to be regarded as a species of nonsense or cognitively meaningless. This is epitomized by Schlick's words when he had it that:

> A theory is a set of hypotheses which may be either true or false by experience... in establishing the identity of meaning and manner of verification we are not making any wonderful discovery, but are pointing to a mere truism[15].

Endorsing Wittgenstein's view that there is a one-to-one correspondence between language and the world, the logical positivists argued that all pronouncements about the absolute, substance, transcendental, theoretical entities, destiny, immortality of the soul, God, supernatural beings, among others, could not be correlated with any substantive entities in the world. As can be seen, all these pronouncements are metaphysical in nature. Thus as a matter of consequence, the logical positivists dismissed metaphysics as a cognitively senseless subject because human mind has had to go beyond the realm of possible experience in order to know and understand it. This apparent hostility and suspicion of metaphysics and the attempt to throw the subject into the dustbin of oblivion by the logical positivists is merely a restatement of previous scholars like Locke, Hume and Comte among others. Recalling Hume's position, he had earlier remarked:

> If we take in our hands any volume; of divinity or school metaphysics for instance, let us ask, does it contain any abstract reasoning concerning quantity or number? No. does it contain any experimental reasoning concerning matter of fact and existence? No, commit it then to the flames; for it can contain nothing but sophistry and illusion [16].

Following from the positivists' (both the earlier and the 1920s positivists) position, it is clear that for them only propositions which can be verified, confirmed or refuted by experience and observation are to be recognized as meaningful; hence their rejection of metaphysics as a subject worth pursuing. But a critical question can still be raised against the positivists: Were positivists right in labelling and dismissing metaphysics as a worthless subject? This is the question we are turning on to in the next section.

The Indispensability of Metaphysics

Given the criticisms levelled against metaphysics by the positivists, it appears unnecessary or rather ridiculous to raise the question on whether metaphysics as a branch of philosophy is of any significance.

In view of this question, I will quickly mention that metaphysics ranks as one of the "core" branches of philosophy together with epistemology, ethics and logic. The word "core" is deliberately used to underscore the point that metaphysics is such a fundamental area of philosophy as distinct from a range of the applied philosophies such as: philosophy of history, philosophy of science, philosophy of religion, philosophy of law, philosophy of medicine/medical ethics and philosophy of education, among others. The intention of comparing metaphysics with the applied philosophies is not to undermine the latter, but rather to show the centrality of metaphysics as a branch of philosophy that feed the applied philosophies.

In view of this it is necessary to point out that no curriculum of philosophy can be said to be complete if it omits metaphysics. So is the curriculum that omits the other core branches of philosophy mentioned above-epistemology, logic and ethics. A quick flashback in history of metaphysics reminds us that metaphysics, called "After Physics" following a posthumous title given to Aristotle's works by Andronicus of Rhodes, had a beginning dating back to the ancient times when the Ionian philosopher scientists reflected on the ultimate stuff or substance of the universe or what is there. The term metaphysics has come to mean the science of being as such and in recent times, it has concerned itself with the investigation into the nature of ultimate reality and raises questions as: What is the essence of being? What is the meaning of life? What is the purpose of man on earth?

It seems no one would dispute the fact that these questions and others of this nature are fundamental to the domain of knowledge, science and life in general. As such denying metaphysics is in itself denying knowledge. Who wants to remain ignorant? If none, then, metaphysics remains a discipline worth pursuing. Thus, with the quest to understand important questions such as those raised above, metaphysicians have always carried on their business unchallenged right from the ancient, through the mediaeval and the early modern period, although, there were disagreements and disputations which is a common feature in philosophy. However, there was a certain conspiracy, as it was, a gang-up in the modern period emanating from the activities of the logical positivists to destroy and erase metaphysics from the compass of philosophy and the domain of knowledge in general. To what extend did they manage to erase metaphysics from the table? This is the question we will grapple with in the next few pages.

Metaphysics a Winner? : A Critical Appraisal

As alluded to in the previous discussion, the positivists wanted to get rid of metaphysics with their "verifiability Principle," but critical analysis of the latter clearly shows that there are some conceptual and linguistic confusion surrounding the principle itself. It is not entirely clear how to verify the principle itself. Yet one may argue if the principle is used as a yardstick to judge or verify other principles, then, it should be verifiable as well. What kind of observations would show that the "verifiable Principle" is wholly true and not false? In other words: Is it possible to verify the principle of verification itself to prove that it is in itself true and meaningful before it is used as a yardstick for other propositions? If not, by what standard can the principle be used to judge and sweep under carpet the existence of disciplines such as metaphysics?

More destructive to the verification principle is the charge of solipsism which tends to threaten the principle. Basing on this criticism, one can note that Schlick's pronouncements that: "if a statement is meaningful to me, it must be verifiable by me"[17], is fatally a drawback to the verification criteria itself. It's self-defeating. This remark did not even go well with other positivists, particularly Neurath and Carnap who, apparently avoiding the subjectivism implicit in Schlick's view claimed that it was not enough to determine the truth of what someone perceives based on someone's experiences, but that his physiological components should be taken into consideration. It does not seem however that this move meets the charge of solipsism levelled against the principle since the danger of episodes of subterfuges by the perceiver cannot be totally eliminated. In any case, positivists themselves failed to adequately justify their position. Their "verifiability principle" is still marred by serious torrents of conceptual and practical problems.

Echoing my argument that metaphysics should receive adequate attention by philosophers and non-philosophers alike, I invoke Rene Descartes who made it clear that scientific advancements of the time did not necessarily mean scientists must give up religion. Neither did it mean philosophers had to give up their philosophical inquiries as those in metaphysics. In anchoring this starts, Descartes made significant contributions to the 17th century scientific revolution primarily by his invention of analytical geometry. His Meditation on First Philosophy (1640) intended to provide both philosophical foundations and a program for the new mathematical physics. In Meditation IV, he even argued that, since God is infinite and incomprehensible to human reason and that since our natures are weak and feeble, we can know nothing of the purposes of God. This implies that the kind of cause – final cause – which has to do with purpose finds no useful employment in physical things. It is to be left aside for metaphysics and not science to pursue.

That said, it is important to underscore that the revolt against metaphysics by positivism (both earlier positivism and the 1920s logical positivism) was a fiasco, a total failure that alone could not erase metaphysics from the horizon. And indeed, the final requiem of the logical positivist movement was song of the time when Schlick was brutally murdered by a frustrated student and other surviving members of the movement immigrated to America, England, and Holland following the Nazi Germany insurgence which was opposed to the radicalism and anti-clericalism of the members of the Circle.

Apart from the unfortunate fate suffered by the members of the Vienna Circle either individually or collectively leading to the eventual collapse of the movement, the logical positivists are accused of making unsubstantiated and dubious epistemological claims that science never uses non-empirical arguments, and that what we regard as metaphysics never draws on empirical premises[18]. Metaphysics sometimes starts its inquiries from the known-the physical-to the unknown.

In light of arguments raised so far in favour of metaphysics, it can be maintained that metaphysics is a fundamentally meaningful inquiry. Other subjects/issues that the subject investigates are also pursued in other scholarly disciplines like science, anthropology, culture, religion and many others. Ayo Fadahunsi resounds this argument in his claim that "both science and metaphysics as human activities attempt to explore and explain the universe as a whole, although, metaphysics goes much deeper than science in raising more general questions bordering on human life and God's existence and man's purpose and relationship with his creator."[19] Thus, I repeat: "denying metaphysics in the domain of knowledge is denying knowledge itself." Yet, it is the challenge posed by the logical positivists to metaphysics that have made the author of this book to look into the history of metaphysics from antiquity before looking at African metaphysical epistemology, which is the core of this book.

I should quickly note, however, that debates on metaphysics (such as those demonstrated in this chapter) take us to another critical question: "Granted that metaphysics is a reality and a subject worth studying; can we also address African metaphysics?" I grant that most of us find it hard to be certain on what to say in response to many metaphysical questions as truth can be a very elusive commodity in metaphysics as in many other fields of inquiry. As such, we might expect there is a sharp disagreement about the question raised above. To address the question, we are naturally led to discuss in some details arguments supporting and opposing African metaphysics and, in light of this, decide whether all things considered, African metaphysics can be a legitimate discipline worth pursuing or rather worth studying in colleges and universities.

Notes

1. Kim, J. and E. Sosa (Eds). A Companion to Metaphysics. London: Blackwell Publishers, 1995.
2. Hamlyn, D.W. Metaphysics. Cambridge: Cambridge University Press, 1984.
3. Ayer AJ. 1981. The Vienna Circle. Midwest Studies in Philosophy, 1: 183.
4. Hamlyn, D.W. Metaphysics. Cambridge: Cambridge University Press, 1984.

5. Jancar, B. The Philosophy of Aristotle, Monarch Press, New York, 1964. pp.90.
6. Bruce Aune, Metaphysics: The Elements, Minneapolis, University of Minnesota Press, 1985, pp.3.
7. Jancar, B. 1964. Op. cit. pp.90.
8. Logical positivism" in Richard A. Popkin (ed.) The Columbia History of Western Philosophy. (New York: Columbia University Press, 1999, pp..621.
9. A. J. Ayer, 1981. The Vienna circle in Midwest Studies in Philosophy. Vol. VI, pp. 183.
10. Logical positivism" in Richard A. Popkin (Ed.).The Columbia History of Western Philosophy. (New York: Columbia University Press, 1999, pp.621.
11. Richard A. Popkin (Ed.). The Columbia History of Western Philosophy. (New York: Columbia University Press, 1999, pp.622.
12. Benjamin R. Tilgman, An Introduction to the Philosophy of Religion, Blackwell: USA, 1994, pp.50.
13. For details on Comte's laws see Ozumba GO. A Resume of the History of Modern and Contemporary Philosophy, in J.D Atemie, N Onuobia (Eds.): Contemporary General Studies, Port-Harcourt: Hereon Investments Ltd., 1994, pp. 512.
14. Oswald Hanfling, "Tractatus, Verificationism and Meaning as Use" in Wittgenstein. The Vienna Circle and Critical Rationalism Proceedings of the Third International Wittgenstein Symposium 13th – 19th august, 1978. pp.78.
15. A. J. Ayer, 1981. Op. cit. pp.182.
16. David Hume, Enquiry Concerning Human Understanding quoted by R. H. Popkin and A. Stroll, Philosophy Made Simple, London: A. Howard and Wyndham Company, 1969, pp. 120.
17. Oswald Hanfling. Op. cit. 1978. pp.78.
18. Edward Craig. "Metaphysics" in Routledge Encyclopedia of Philosophy, London and Canada: Routledge, 1998, pp. 338-340.
19. Fadahunsi Ayo. The Metaphysical Foundation of Science. In: Dipo Irele (Ed.): Philosophy. Logic and Scientific Reasoning. Ibadan: New Horn Press, 1999, pp. 116.

Chapter Two

Uncovering African Metaphysics

The subject of African metaphysics is a very broad and far reaching inquiry. In any case, there are two strategic hurdles to overcome. First, is how we can meaningfully talk about African metaphysics as an independent philosophical discipline? Second, is whether it is possible to cover the breadth and depth of African metaphysics in totality? Perhaps the consoling goad is the fact that no work can claim to say all that needs be said (in terms depth and breadth) on any subject matter. What is important in any given work is to have a clear vision of what is intended to be achieved.

There is no one universal way of defining African metaphysics, but what I can do here is to provide a minimal guide for the idea of African metaphysics. That what is distinctively African in African metaphysics today derives from African traditional thought. Kwasi Wiredu is driving at this point when he observes that the conceptions of the African people, as a cultural group, on being, reality, God, the universe, as they grapple with the natural and supernatural entities in their environment are generally alike[1]. This understanding is based on the belief that any group of human beings will certainly need to have some world outlook, that is, some general conceptions about the world in which they live and about themselves both as individuals and collectively as members of the same society. Having the same understanding of Africa and the African people, Ozumba[2] defines African metaphysics as "the African way of perceiving, interpreting and making meaning out of interactions, among beings, and reality in general". It is the totality of the African's perception of reality. This will embrace the holistic conception of reality with its appurtenance of relations, qualities, characterizations, being and its subtleties universals, particular, ideas, minds, culture, logic, moral, theories and presuppositions. I have cited Wiredu and Ozumba's definitions above at the risk of being accused of relativism. Nevertheless, it is important to emphasize that the issues dealt with in metaphysics, whether African metaphysics or Western metaphysics are universal. What is different is how each culture treats and understands these issues as metaphysical issues are contingent on the values and cultures of the people in question. It is this crucial characteristic that distinguishes African metaphysics from western metaphysics. This is captured and underscored in the Belgian missionary, Placide Tempels' claim that whereas the western people hold a static conception of being and maintain a certain detachment with the object, the African people hold a dynamic conception of being[3]. It is also premised on the claim by Teffo and Roux that "reality is seen as a closed system so that everything hangs together and is affected by any change in the system"[4]. The change can be variation within cultures, especially in the Western and African cultures.

Recalling what has been said of African metaphysics by Temples, it can be remarked that the conception of reality in African metaphysics is holistic, interrelated and pragmatic. In fact if an idea, an explanation or a belief works, it is accepted even though it may not fulfil certain criteria of defining objective reality such as empirical validation. The logic of African metaphysics thus underpins the African standards and expectations. This is not to go with the impression that all African communities share the same standard even though the standard is community based. Borrowing from Willard V. O. Quine, each community operates from a background theory that penetrates its perception and metaphysics of reality. If you see things other than the way the community sees them, they will demean your understanding and systematize with your "alienness". What I mean here is that Africans have a common general orientation and perception of reality. They have an important component to their conception of reality, a domain whose existence is explained mystically and not empirically. This is one of the Africans' strongest beliefs in their cosmology. This belief has also influenced their understanding of reality as a composite of matter and spirit either co-existing or existing as separate entities. As such, Africans have a hierarchy of existence with God at the pinnacle followed by the ancestors in their perking order of seniority and down to the living beings-human beings still in their biological bodies. There is ample evidence among Africans that the activities of the ancestors and God affect people in various ways whether positively or adversely; hence the need to revere them.

Following the Africans' conception of hierarchy of existence is the concept of "causation". To the Africans, the concept of causality is central to their metaphysics. It is predicated on the maxim that there is no effect without a cause and no action or reality may bring itself into existence. Even though Africans are aware of purely scientific causal explanations, they do not often consider them as profound enough to offer complete satisfaction in accounting for the events of life that they feel need another explanation – the supernatural causation – besides the scientific one. This leads them to give up on the search for empirical causal explanations, even of causal relations between natural phenomena, or events and resort to supernatural causation. Thus, the African people's faith in agentive causality leads them to postulate mystical powers as causal agents to events in this world, positive and negative, scientific and non-scientific.

The puzzle of how the immaterial spiritual entities come to interact and continue to influence the activities of the living does not arise for the Africans as it does for those who subscribe to the scientific laws or mechanistic view of the world from a Western orientation. However, the African idea of causality is not difficult to understand once one has understood the fact that Africans believe in immortality of the soul and in the existence of spiritual beings. The ancestors, for example, did not die but passed on to the next world; they are in the world beyond and can still come back to interact with those in the physical world. As enunciated by Tempels[5] the Bantu - Africans believe that "vital force is even more than a necessary attribute of beings: force is the nature of being, force is being, and being is force". It is only by fortifying their vital force – force vitale (spirit) – through the use of magical recipes and through praying to the ancestors and pouring libation that they acquire resistance to malevolent external forces. Failure to observe this would imply exposing oneself to danger by giving up on the security that is guaranteed by the ancestors and God. Spiritual beings thus are very much counted among the living as important participants in shaping everything that may happen and by their very nature they now occupy a better position in determining events and influencing them. They enjoy this position as they are no longer believed to be subject to the limitations of space and time. And for this reason among others, the spirits are believed to be versatile and unpredictable and so are always revered and treated with great caution. Their "tamper" can no longer be determined easily and evil-minded people (the witches and wizards) can manipulate them such that they turn against members of their own lineage and cause havoc. This is why, throughout Africa, sick or afflicted people go to consult diviners to explain the causes of their troubles. Usually the answer they get involves some spiritual agency of some sort. Reference to theoretical entities is used to link events in the visible, tangible world (natural effects) to their antecedents in the same world (natural causes). The diviner as one who can directly interact with the spirits basically transcends the limited vision of natural causes provided by common sense.

It is of the greatest importance to note that though African metaphysics is not rooted in the analytic tradition of western philosophy, this does not render it less rigorous. African metaphysics in the primeval period due to their unwritten nature cannot provide us with a written rigorous specimen of the metaphysics argumentation and analysis unique to Africa. Nonetheless, the spirit of rigour is not absent because every view is carefully examined before accepted and used to rationally explain a cosmic puzzle. This is one reason why I have already highlighted in the preceding discussion that Africans have a pragmatic metaphysics- a metaphysics that is acceptable only if it fulfils certain (though not all) fundamental criteria of objective reality. If an idea works, the Africans still dig deep to unravel through mystical means to ascertain the basis for such phenomenon in their reality scheme. This means that the Africans are aware of the consequences of superficial contemplation of their universe. They think and try as deeply and rigorous as their theoretical and experiential apparatus could aid them. Not having a form of writing must have hindered serious reflective afterthought which ruminating over written experiences can afford. A mere mental acquaintance with reality cannot guarantee tenacity and longevity of ideas. The ideas evaporate or fly away and new attempts should always be made from time to time to recapture the substance of previous experience. This could be therefore registered as the limitations of African traditional metaphysical thought systems. Critics thus can charge African metaphysics with being less rigorous for nothing is accepted without "written" evidence and reason. The reason may commit us to either empirical or rational validation. However, Africans realized these limitations and possible critics and devised ways to surpass and do away with the limitations. As Omoregbe has rightly pointed out, "the Africans store their ideas in form of folklores, folk wisdom, mythologies, traditional proverbs, religious world views, etc. This enables them to examine more closely their views"[6]. Of course, this form of preservation cannot be compared with thoughts in written form. However, through the above-stated literary genres Africans' experiences were logically tested in order to ascertain their truth. These tests provided the Africans with rational clues as they continue their forays into the wilderness of reality.

This mirrors my argument that in African metaphysics, empiricism merges with rationalism. It involves a synthesis of all experiences in order to achieve a coherent whole which gives a complete picture of reality. The cleavage between empiricism and rationalism, if it exists at all, is not a matter for serious epistemological dispute. With this background, we are obliged to examine how African metaphysics just like Western metaphysics has evolved through time from mythological metaphysics to logical metaphysics. This is in order to see how the disparate metaphysical objects of the Africans fit into a coherent metaphysical framework.

African Metaphysics' Struggle for Recognition

Notwithstanding its shortcomings, mythological African metaphysics has served a very important function in the development of logical metaphysics in Africa as elsewhere in the world. Mythological African metaphysics has created a fertile ground for the realization of important psychological and moral needs of the individual and community at large. It is a metaphysics that has been instrumental and fundamentally important to the Africans in tackling problematic issues of African society. As such, mythological African metaphysics has been crucial to questions of moral cohesion, epistemology, social control, law and order within African societies. Yet, it remains paramount to examine how this metaphysics operated in Africa, and why it was necessary to develop to what I shall call "logical African metaphysics".

On the basis of African mythological metaphysics, questions concerning life issues concentrated much on providing answers to the practical questions and problems of the day. Though this is a worthwhile aspect of African mythological metaphysics this method has however failed, in most cases, to give satisfactory answers in such areas as prediction and control of diseases, hunger, natural catastrophes, and climatic and cosmic changes, among other problems. It has also failed to give room to individual African metaphysicians to fully develop their potentialities and offer lasting solutions and answers to our day to day problems. Knowledge or rather mythological metaphysical beliefs are collective. Thus as long as the approach to questions posed in these areas is enclosed within a casual framework explicable mostly by recourse to the activities of mythological and magical forces, there would hardly be any appreciable progress towards understanding, mastering and giving satisfactory and adequate solutions to them. The same could be said of attempts at understanding and explaining human destiny which is fundamental to socio-economic welfare of the individual and community. Mythologically-based metaphysics sees these areas largely as something that is beyond the control of man and so beyond human comprehension. Under such as scenario, group dynamics is hardly understandable and explicable merely on the basis of rules governing organizations and peoples, or rules derivable from interpersonal relations within a society. Thus the tendency of metaphysical epistemology to postulating non-rational schemes as the principles governing actions and intentions of individuals in groups and societies is rendered futile. So is its recourse to charms, magical and occult manipulative means as substitute for explanations based on clear cut scientific inspiration. The idea of magical manipulation of people in decision making processes, for example, defies the fundamental principles of group dynamics that is won through testable and tested models and principles relating to group activities. On the basis of postulation of the idea of spiritual forces, medium, mystical empowerment through use of charms, occult practices, magical manipulations, medicine men a mythological metaphysics that dwells on resolving only practical questions could end up being utopian and technically inconsequential; hence there is always need (in Africa as elsewhere) to go beyond mythological metaphysics to logical/rational metaphysics.

Also, since it falls within the grasp of African metaphysical thinking, mythological African metaphysics would readily fall within the area of the mysterious, magical and the occult; it is worth noting that mythological metaphysics is empirically and humanly unattainable. This way, possibilities to break new grounds are compromised because metaphysics is wrongly conceived as serving merely an incomplete super-sensible function. In essence, the courage to break new grounds without appearing mythological or magical is one of the hall marks of the philosophical metaphysics, African metaphysics included.

Realizing such short-comings of mythological African metaphysics, African metaphysicians (through the mouthpiece of African philosophy) have always worked tirelessly to see to it that African metaphysics is evolved and refined along with time. Contemporary African metaphysicians are preoccupied with the task of explaining the nature, scope and drafting ways of integrating African metaphysics in the mainstream philosophy so that African metaphysics be recognized as an independent philosophical discipline that can be studied in universities and colleges. The desire of contemporary metaphysicians to have this dream realized is seen in the way African scholars have recently devoted themselves in philosophical writings and have improved their interacting horizons with their environment and the world. When looking at different kinds of theoretical debates on Africa held in several academic journals, it is striking how many articles especially from the African scholars (living within Africa or abroad), focus on African metaphysics or African philosophy in general. This harmonious interaction of the African scholars with their environment and the world through writing or otherwise is not something accidental, but something within, logical and rational. It is something rooted in a logical metaphysics that for a long time have been forced by mythological prejudices to remain within and indeed silent. And, this break away is a necessary condition for African metaphysics to be recognized as legitimate philosophical discipline equal to other western philosophical disciplines.

It is a truism that in African metaphysics the spirits, the concomitant and ancillary cosmic forces have always served not only as instances of arbitration, punishment but instances of reward in our relationship with the world. They are evoked when necessary and avoided when dangerous. It is the role of contemporary African metaphysicians to explain to the world the mystical complex relationships of the Africans with their environment (physical or otherwise). It is undeniable that Africans' relationship with their environment is borne not only out of the intellectual curiosity to know their nature, essence and mode of existence but out of man's personal relationship to these forces as sources of regulation of social and individual conflicts; that the influence of these forces was felt beyond the world of human existence shows itself in the African understanding of the influence of these forces on all conditions necessary for a meaningful life. What remains difficult for many however is to understand the complex relationships and nature of the "forces" that are said to regulate the essence and mode human existence in African cosmology. It is this challenge, among others, that has made African metaphysics hardly recognized as a philosophical discipline. I will not delve into these debates here and now. We will look at the subject in some detail in the ensuing chapters. I think it might be helpful however to submit that African metaphysics has been the guarantor of the African understanding of community life as a co-operate affair since it creates the precondition for understanding of social cohesion based on people's alignment and allegiance to particular metaphysical forces that give meaning collectively to their lives and actions. This conception about the community has been one of the important factors that have guaranteed the continued survival of African people in the face of untold economic and social difficulties and hardship. This type of metaphysics sustains the psyche of the individual who relegates his absolute confidence to forces whose loyalty can be guaranteed through man's religious and cultic obligations to them. African metaphysicians thus should continue working to ensure that African metaphysics is totally liberated from mythological metaphysics. As it still stands, African metaphysics is still largely linked to mythological metaphysics. It seems the major reason for this persistent connection of African metaphysics to mythological metaphysics it the strong connection of the former to African traditional culture. The section below therefore unveils that which is beneath African traditional culture.

Beneath African Traditional Culture

African traditional culture is the wellspring of African philosophy, African metaphysics included. And, African traditional culture originates from the interaction of the Africans with nature. One more thing to note is that beneath the African traditional culture is the African traditional religion which in itself inspires African philosophy. The trio (African traditional religion, African traditional culture and African philosophy) are closely intertwined. This is one reason why I have argued in the section above that African metaphysics like western metaphysics is born out of mythological metaphysics. Let us examine the relationship of the trio together and see how we can push forward what is logically metaphysical and improve and liberate that which is still enshrouded in metaphysical mythology.

Metaphysics in general terms deals with first principles and seeks to explain the nature of "being" or reality, and ontology. Given that many religions, African traditional religions included, deal with explanations and beliefs about reality and ontology, religions qualify as metaphysics. There is no reason, whatsoever, that can bar religious issues from being considered as metaphysical, but of course, as religious metaphysics. The strong bond between African religions and philosophy is supported by John Mbiti who rightly points out that "Africans are notoriously religious and religion is part and parcel of the African heritage which goes back many thousands of years."[7] This suggests that Africans are notoriously metaphysical though not in a purely philosophical sense of spectators and speculators, but as practitioners. This is one reason why traditionalists in the African continent vehemently oppose the rapid spread of western values and lifestyles in Africa. They see them as detrimental to what they cherish in their culture, especially attitudes and customs related to their metaphysical beliefs. Father Tempels echoes the same sentiments when he argues that those who refuse to acknowledge the existence of black thought exclude blacks from the group of human beings.

African religion is the basis and the mirror of the African people's existence. It is their life. This is encapsulated even in their proverbs, among other literary genres, religion is a coherent theory that constructs and corresponds to African thought, expression and customs where people extract fundamental ideas from them. Africa as her western counterpart knows how to philosophize. Through languages that are full of figures of speech and also the spirit of ubuntu (humanness) which is at the heart of African traditional religion, Africans are able to distinguish the right from the wrong, the bad from the good. They are also able to formulate their metaphysical and epistemological assertions. Mogobe Ramose defines this mega aptitude as "the root of African philosophy" and of course, African metaphysics. Ramose furthers to point that the being of an African in the universe is "inseparably anchored upon ubuntu...Ubuntu then is the wellspring flowing with African ontology and epistemology."[8] This is to say that philosophy as with religion for Africans is embedded in their day to day practices and language that are crucial aspects of their lives that includes activities like birth occasions of a child, giving of names, marriage, funerals, harvesting festivals, rain making prayers, circumcision and other initiation ceremonies, to mention a few. Affirming the view that religious symbols, objects, art, dance, music, proverbs, folklore, riddles, idioms and wise sayings manifest religious expressions, John Mbiti succinctly puts it that:

> Because traditional religions permeate all the departments of life, there is no formal distinction between the sacred and the secular, between the religious and the nonreligious, between

the spiritual and the material areas of life. Wherever the African is, there is his religion: he carries it to the field where he is sowing seeds or harvesting a new crop; he takes it with him to the beer party or to attend a funeral ceremony....[9]

The recognition of the root of African philosophy and indeed the need to reclaim reason for Africa have resulted in some African like Ngugi wa Thiongo advocating for decolonization of the African mind whose consciousness and culture were for a moment submerged and tampered with by the western colonialism. Decolonization of the African mind after national liberations aimed not only at liberation of the process of development of national productive forces. It also aimed at liberating Africans' consciousness and fosters their ability to determine the mode of production that is most appropriate to their own evolution. For Ngugi and rightly so, this is necessary (even today) given that the westerners viewed Africa as a dark continent devoid of any history, culture and worse still philosophy. Africa was denied a culture in the process and this served as an ideological licensing of exploitation, subjugation and colonialism. There is therefore need for Africans to go back to their culture where their philosophy and religious aspirations are buried.

Other Africans like Molefi Kete Asante echoed the same sentiments on Africa and for Africans. He cited in Mengara, notes that national liberation of the African nations was against a certain socio-historic context that Hegel wrote in 1828: "Let us forget Africa, for it is no part of human history."[10] The Diop-Olela tradition, also opposed to the Hegelian bias quotes from George James's The Stolen Legacy in Masolo who neatly remarks:

> Now that it has been shown that philosophy and science were bequeathed to civilization by the people of...Africa and not by the people of Greece, the pendulum of praise and honour is due to shift from the people of Greece to the people of the African continent...that the Greeks were not the authors of Greek philosophy, but the people of Africa.[11]

All these sentiments by African scholars have been tested and tried in time. They conclusively reinforce the idea that Africa is the cradle of all civilization; hence shutters the false pride of some western scholars whose works have injured many African scientists and researchers' consciousness and culture.

The Continued Relevance of African Metaphysics

The distinction between metaphysics as body of beliefs and metaphysics as a fundamental science or rather as a tool of exploration, among others, has incidentally been the root of most harsh and destructive criticisms against metaphysics,[12] (African metaphysics included), as a quest in futility. African metaphysics in particular has been criticized together with African philosophy for being deeply rooted in culture and for operating in a manner that contrasts with the understanding of metaphysics as a tool for science motivated explanation of reality. African metaphysics, which largely takes the form of a set or body of beliefs and practices in relation to the ultimate reality, thus has been considered as the mythological model of metaphysics rather than metaphysics per se. This is because the dynamic constitution of nature, whose self-explanatory force is fundamental for scientific growth, is replaced by belief in a dynamic force in the form of a personal god, spirit or other agencies responsible for explanation of the reality of things. This model of metaphysics concentrates primarily in grasping the nature of the "being" responsible for the existence of the world; it is comfortable with taking stock of the very attribute of this "personal being," his relationship with man and nature.

Even in the face of these criticisms and others highlighted in the previous discussions, African metaphysics remains relevant though in a manner that contrasts with the understanding of metaphysics as a tool for science motivated explanation of reality. Omeregbe highlights an important dimension of African traditional metaphysics as it relates to the explanation of the ultimate nature of things. For him within African context there are mystical or supernatural forces which defy any scientific analysis or explanation. These forces surpass and sometimes counteract physical (scientific) forces. They can be manipulated by man and employed for both good and evil purposes, such as protection, prevention of calamities, cure of diseases, procreation and bringing about sickness, death, and other kinds of misfortune to people[13]. While I agree with Omeregbe, I go beyond his position and further argue that in a case as this (of African metaphysics) consistent, systematic and modest in-depth inquiry concerning the mechanisms inherent in the constitution of things themselves remain necessary for an African metaphysician. If African metaphysicians manage to explain these complexities enshrouding African metaphysics – difficulties which neither western metaphysics nor science has managed to explain – certainly, African metaphysics will be declared a universal winner and maintains its front seat position as the most basic and thorough inquiry of all human endeavours. An African metaphysician thus has the task to explain in a logical and cogent manner how manipulation of some forces in African metaphysics is possible. With this goal, African metaphysics (like metaphysics in general) remains a catalyst of scientific progress and exploration. This is borne from the insight that scientific progress is sustained by the urge to go beyond each attainable result. This urge is inspired by metaphysics alone and no other discipline. This fact remains a consoling goad and pride of African metaphysics and metaphysics in general.

Besides, the knowledge and understanding of concepts such as ancestors, supernatural beings, among many others in the realm of African metaphysics, would not have been possible if African metaphysics had been obliterated from the compass of philosophical discourse on the basis that it contrasts with the understanding of metaphysics as a tool for science motivated explanation of reality. African metaphysics like metaphysics in general, thus, is still a live and critical philosophical discipline. This is captured by Innocent Onyewuenyi, quoting Henry Alpern, who correctly utters:

> Metaphysics is necessary for art, morality, religion, economics and sociology, for the abstract sciences as well as every branch of human endeavour considered from the practical angle. Even science or scientific knowledge cannot be said to be totally experiential. For there contain, within its system,

certain unobservable entities like proton, electron and electromagnetic waves[14].

This renders futile the rejection of African metaphysics or the attempt to purge it of all spiritualistic and supra-sensible entities that are not accessible to empirical verification or whose scrutiny is preposterous. In any case, both African metaphysics (as metaphysics in general) and science attempt to explain reality by a priori principles.

However, the justification for the relevance and necessary existence of African metaphysics should not be interpreted as saying that African metaphysicians must fold their arms and do nothing to further develop the subject. African metaphysicians should not be contended by the fact that African metaphysics is surrounded with mystery and unobservable entities. Instead, the mysteries and complexities surrounding African metaphysics should always remain as a source of inspiration and intellectual courage for an African metaphysician to move forward in trying to understand, dismantle and explain fully to the world. Such attempts remain a necessary challenge for all African metaphysicians, both operating within or outside Africa. This is a serious call to African metaphysicians. Otherwise, African metaphysics will never be recognized as a philosophical discipline but rather as a mythological model of metaphysics. This book was indeed born out of such an inspiration and quest: to explain African metaphysics from within, not without.

Yet even after justifying the relevance of African metaphysics, all good inquiring minds would no doubt want to know whether it is compatible with western metaphysics? This is the question we will discuss in the next section.

The Compatibility of African and Western Metaphysics

Is there any relationship between western metaphysics and African metaphysics? Or to what extent are they compatible? These two questions are one and the same. They both point to the common ground of western and African metaphysics if any.

The above stated questions can be answered in various ways. I shall explore the question using the philosophical concept of "essence" (of things) which is common in both African metaphysics and western metaphysics. This is done in order to see how "essence" is conceived in both African metaphysics and western metaphysics. I have chosen this concept because it is commonplace in all cultures, African or otherwise. In this book, the concept "essence" shall be used interchangeably with the concept "nature". This is not to be taken to mean that I am not aware of the differences between "nature" and "essence" that Aristotle mentioned in his Physics, Book 2. The use of this concept in this book has been facilitated by the fact that the two concepts are generally understood to refer to one and the same thing in the subject of philosophy; though metaphysically some lines of difference between them can be drawn.

Technically, essence signifies something common to all things (natures) through which various "beings" are placed in the various genera and species: the universal[15]. A fine example given by Avicenna is "humanness" which he rightly said is the essence of all human beings; it is common to all things referred to as human beings. Put it differently, essence means what it is to be a particular thing-the "whatness" or "quintessence" of a thing.

Now coming back to our subject, one would notice that in African metaphysics the essence or nature of all things is conceived as "vital force"- force vitale- heretofore referred to as force. Western metaphysics conceive the essence of all things to be "substance". Thus while in African metaphysics "force" is the essential nature of things, "substance" is the term used to signify that which is sought when philosophers investigate the primary being of things (substance-ousia) or essential nature. In Western metaphysics, substance is conjoined with the notion of accidents, which are predicable features of the essence of a being. Accidents may change or disappear, while substance always remains unaltered; they are eternal. I shall not venture into the Aristotelian and Scholastic discussions of proper, essential and logical accidents. I will rush to emphasize that in western metaphysics, man is made up of substance and accidents; the substance is the soul or the spirit; the accident is the body or matter. In Cartesian language, man is a mind/body dualism.

From our discussion of essence in western metaphysics, one would notice that this understanding makes little or no difference with that found in African metaphysics. Adding to the earlier treatment of the African concept of being as "vital force" and its dynamic nature, it can be advanced that in the category of visible beings Africans distinguish that which is perceived by the senses and the "thing in itself" namely: the inner nature which is the "force" of the thing whether man, animal, tree and the body. The "force" like substance (in western metaphysics) in that it is eternal and unalterable. When a person dies, for example, African traditionalists do not say that the "vital force-soul" of the dead has gone to the spiritual world. It is not the "vital force/soul" or "part of man" that has gone to the world of the spirits but the whole man though not in a visible but invisible state. This is because what is considered as "the man" - thing in itself - is the inner force, not the outer body. Tempels captures this when he explains:

> What lives on after death is not called by the Bantu by a term indicating part of man. I have always heard their elders speak of "the man himself"; or it is "the little man" who was formerly hidden behind the perceptible manifestation of the man; or muntu which at death has left the living. Muntu signifies vital force endowed with intelligence and will[16].

It can be noted from Temples' remark that the "force" doesn't die, but only leaves the living (which can be understood to be the body). This understanding is also pervasive in western metaphysics where the "substance" which is understood to be unchanging and eternal is comparable to the force vitale. Similarly, the accidents which can change or disappear are comparable to the body. Thus drawing on the earlier example of a man, western metaphysics would say the body (of the man) as an accident may change, rot, and cease at death, but the substance-soul, spirit, mind- the essence that is, (for man) subsists. Though in African metaphysics, the dichotomy of "soul" and "body" is not applicable such that at death, the soul separates and inhabits another body, "the man" still exists as this person in a spiritual invisible form. His bodily energy goes but his vital force persists and waxes stronger and stronger ontologically. The question of immortality of the "force" or soul (to use Western junction) thus is not a controversial issue in African reality scheme as it is in Western metaphysics. It is a truism. The force-soul of a man is immortal. It continues to exist after the dissolution of the body. What remains paramount in both western metaphysics and African metaphysics is the fact that both the force (soul) and essence (substance) are eternal and so persist after dissolution of the physical body. This common understanding in African metaphysics and Western metaphysics is clear testimony that the two are agreeable or rather compatible.

It is of the greatest importance to remember that while both African metaphysics and western metaphysics concur that all things have essential nature, they differ on the name they attribute to this nature; "force" and "substance" respectively. In addition, while substance is conjoined with the notion of accidents, the vital force can be hardly distinguished from the thing itself, that is, from that which exists-"being". For this reason it is even wrong to say that "being" in the African thought has the necessary element or quality of force. The precision of the Africans' concept of being will not be attained if their notion of "being" is expressed as "being is that which possesses force". Instead, the concept of force in African metaphysics is therefore inseparable from the definition of "being" itself. There is no idea among Africans of "being" divorced from the idea of "force". This is to mean that without the element "vital force," "being" cannot be conceived since force is the nature of being- "force is being and being is force"[17]. One should be cautious, however, not to confuse this dynamic notion of essence with some kind of universal force common to all existing things. African metaphysics clearly distinguish between different essences of beings, just as there are different categories of material entities. It is at this point that African metaphysics differs from western metaphysics when it comes to the concept of essence. For example, in terms of western metaphysics, beings are differentiated by their essences or nature. Yet, in African metaphysics it is the forces that differ in their essences or nature to the extent that there are: "the divine force, terrestrial or celestial forces, human forces, and vegetable and even mineral forces"[18]. These forces, depending on the differences in their essence or nature, these forces follow a hierarchical order such that God precedes the spirits; then come the founding fathers and the living-dead, according to the order of primogeniture; then the living according to their rank in terms of seniority.

As demonstrated above, African metaphysics and western metaphysics can be said to be compatible though they seem to attribute different names to the essential nature of things and other such concepts. This is chiefly because of differences in culture and orientation. Otherwise, with the concept of essence African and western metaphysics quest to explain the same thing; both metaphysics seek to understand the underlying reality of things. Besides, there are many other concepts commonplace in both African and western metaphysics. These include God, soul/spirit, life, death, love, beauty, and time, among others. Metaphysicians, not only from the African and western cultures, but also other cultures tussle with various aspects of these concepts.

One question, however, remains critical: Is the analysis made so far on African metaphysics right? It is likely that some readers will doubt that it is. And, this is expected of all philosophical minds. To decide whether this suspicion is well founded, we need to look more closely at the African ontology and concepts found in African metaphysics. It is to the subject of the nature of being or reality (ontology) through analysis of concepts common in African metaphysics that we turn next.

Notes

1. Kwasi Wiredu, "On Defining African Philosophy," in Tsenay Serequeberhan (Ed). African Philosophy: The Essential Readings, New York: Paragon House, 1991, pp. 87.
2. Ozumba G. O. 2004. African Traditional Metaphysics, Quodlibet Journal, Vol. 6:3.

3. Tempels Placide. Bantu Philosophy Paris: Presence Africaine, 1969, pp.153.
4. Teffo LJ, Roux APJ. "Metaphysical Thinking in Africa," in PH Coetzee, APJ Roux (Eds.): The African Philosophy Reader. London and New York: Rutledge, 1998, pp. 138.
5. Placide Tempels, Bantu Philosophy, Paris, Présence Africaine, 1959, pp.51.
6. Joseph Omoregbe, Metaphysics without Tears, a Systematic and Historical Study, Nigeria, Joja Educational Research and Publishers Ltd., 1998, pp.5.
7. Mbiti, J.S. An Introduction to African Religion, London: Heinemann. 1975, pp.12.
8. Ramose, M.B. African philosophy through Ubuntu, Harare: Mond Books. 1999, pp.230.
9. Mbiti, J.S. (1969) African Religion and Philosophy. New York: Anchor.pp.2.
10. Hegel cited in Mengara, D.M. (Ed) Images of Africa: Stereotypes and Realities. Trenton and Asmara : Africa world Press. 2001, pp. xiv.
11. George James cited in Masolo, D.A. African Philosophy in Search of Identity, Nairobi: East African Educational Publishers. 1995. pp.21.
12. Kenneth F. Dougherty, Metaphysics, New York 1965, pp. 14.
13. Omoregbe Joseph. Epistemology: A Systematic and Historical Study, Lagos: Joja Educational Research and Publisher Ltd., 1998, pp. 26.
14. Henry Alpern cited in Innocent C. Onyewuenyi, African Belief in Reincarnation: A Philosophical Reappraisal, Enugu: Snaap Press Ltd., 1996, pp. 30.
15. For details on the discussion on Essence and Nature, see Avicenna in Aristotle's Metaphysicae.
16. Tempels Placide 1969. Bantu Philosophy Paris: Presence Africaine, pp.55.
17. Tempels Placide. Ibid. pp.37.
18. Tempels Placide. Ibid. pp.58.

Chapter Three

Ontology and Concepts in African Metaphysics

Metaphysical questions arise when we turn attention from natural science statements to statements concerning religious beliefs. It is in this case that we quickly encounter questions concerning ontology and questions concerning analysis of ontological issues. Ontological issues are those that have something to do with reality/being or existence. As given by William Carter, "we are addressing ontological issues when we ask whether something is real or whether something exists"[1]. Ontology thus is a branch of metaphysics that studies existence of things, both material and immaterial things. To illustrate this, a number of questions that are ontological in nature are given below:

a). Does God exist?
b). What is God if does exist?
c). Are numbers such as 30 or 4 real?
d). Is there any other world besides this in which human beings live?
e). Are there spiritual beings/entities such as angels?
f). Is there any other life after bodily death?
g). Do persons exist?

These and many others of the same nature are commonly asked questions, not only in western metaphysics but also in African metaphysics. All the above questions are posed to either affirm or negate existence or non-existence of certain kind of things. To say that there are persons is the same as that persons exist. And to say that there is no God is the same as saying God does not exist. Some people believe that God exists in reality. Others believe that God only exists in people's minds. Conceivably someone might take the same view when it comes to the question of life after bodily death or spiritual beings such as angels and other such supernatural beings. It is curious to note that whatever position one is going to take, there is need to explain the claim in a rational and convincing manner, if the claimed is to be believed as true and justified. This is because ontological questions are closely tied to questions of analysis-questions which need one to rationally understand what sort of thing a person is, for example, before judging whether persons exist or not. The same would apply to questions that have to do with spiritual beings, numbers, God and life after death/afterlife. We can hardly expect a consensus on the ontological questions raised above as all others unless we first of all understand what the questions themselves mean. It is important at this juncture therefore to point that ontological questions have boggled human mind since time immemorial and have resulted in the formulation of concepts by people in a bid to explain them. I define concept as an abstract thing[2]–it is an idea or at least close relative of idea. This is to suggest that concepts like qualities (of things) are not substantial entities themselves and cannot exist independently. For this reason, one can indeed wonder what to reply with certitude if asked questions: a) and b) above until encounter a God. Questions of this sort are many in African metaphysics as in metaphysics in general. This is one reason that makes African metaphysics (like western metaphysics) controversial and philosophically difficult to unpack. In the next section, we will attempt to unravel some of the ontological issues that are critical in African metaphysics and indeed in metaphysics in general.

The Concept of Being in African Metaphysics

The concept of "being" like any philosophical concept is confusingly difficult to define with precision. However, "being" has been technically defined as a generic term used to represent all existing things – it is anything in the realm of existence-material or immaterial. Conceding with this general sense of the term, McInerny defines "being" as what is, that which exists, reality[3]. We shall not plunge into debates in Western philosophy concerning "being". My task here is to unravel the concept of "being" from an African metaphysical perspective, to explain how "being" is traditionally conceived by Africans.

When the subject of "being" is looked at from an African metaphysics standpoint, one can observe that the term is conceived to mean everything that is; "being" is everything that exists. Africans understand "being" in this sense for the simple reason that there is nothing that exists that is taken lightly and for granted in the African culture. The general belief is that there is reason to be for whatever is. Though man may not immediately know why this or that thing was created for and what really the thing is, all things serve a purpose in one way or another. For Africans, therefore, "being" is therefore conceived as the whole range of existent things. All good inquiring minds would no doubt want to know the existent things; to itemize the existent things alluded to. It is at this point that existent things are grouped into two major categories namely: "material beings" and "immaterial beings" or "spiritual beings". African metaphysics tends to prioritize and pay more regard to the immaterial being; hence the latter shall receive more attention in this book.

As highlighted earlier in this chapter on the discussion on "beings" in African metaphysics, Africans talk of a hierarchy; a hierarchy of "beings". In this hierarchy, all "beings" in the realm of existence participate. However, the intensity of participation differs resulting in some "beings" found at the top of the hierarchy and others at the bottom of the hierarchy. This is to say in African metaphysics, "beings" are classified according to their degree of participation. The immaterial beings are found at the top of the hierarchy and the material beings at the bottom. This also implies superiority of immaterial beings over material beings in the African metaphysics. Yet even among the immaterial beings themselves, there are beings that are superior to others. In the hierarchy of immaterial beings thus is God at the apex. Below God follows the ancestors, particularly national or clan ancestors then, family ancestors. After the family ancestors are the totems or emblems of hereditary relationship followed. Below the totems come other spirits that are manipulated by people in sorcery, witchcraft or magic for certain ends. These are represented at times as charms and amulets, then, we have man and finally, animals and plants as occupying the lowest level[4].

There is the argument in some quarters that this hierarchy is not rigid; it can sometimes be altered. In some cases, events can cause a hitherto insignificant god to become so powerful that it assumes a central place of reverence in the life of the community more than the ancestors. The ancestors are revered because it is held that they are always better disposed to the good of the living. But other gods or divinities are highly capricious and unpredictable that they can manipulate the ancestors and take the positions they occupy in the hierarchy. Plants and animals can be habited by powerful forces which make them to become very prominent in the spiritual rating of the society. This conception of "being" from the point of view of force is pervasive in African conception of "being". This realization may have prompted prominent African philosophers like Tempels to concentrate his attention on this aspect to the neglect of other elements involved in explaining the concept of "being". Henri Maurier[5] in a similar vein has confirmed the vitalist-force vitale framework as most appropriate in understanding the African conception of "being". Vitalist here is seen in the sense of understanding being in terms of force and interrelationship among these forces and the "beings" in the realm of existence.

    This picture will give the impression of a disordered universe of perennial strife among the forces. Though there is, but this strife is controlled and regulated by the unseen hand of the creator which most African cultures agree is God (to use the English word). Africans believe that whatever happens cannot go unnoticed by the omnipresent eyes of the creator. God being at the apex of the hierarchy of "beings" as has been seen above oversees and regulates what goes on in the universe. God's supreme position is unaltered. This quite clear in the African names attributed to God. The Shona and Ndebele (of Zimbabwe), for instance call God Mwari or Musiki and uMlimu respectively meaning "the creator of everything/He who is". The Shanganas of Mozambique call God Xikwembo meaning "father of everything in the realm of existence". For the Zulu, Chewa/Nyanja, Bemba, Tswana and Swahili (of South Africa, Malawi, Zambia, Botswana and the Eastern African Coast respectively) it's Nkulunkulu (the Most high), Chiuta/Chaunta, Lesa (Most high), Modimbo (the Great Being) and Mngu respectively. The Igbo[6] call God Okaka-Amasi-Amasi and Chukwuokike meaning "one who is not fully known, and the creator of the universe". The Yorubas call Him Olodumare meaning "the Almighty God," while the Akan people of Ghana call Him Onyame which means "the Supreme Being". As can be seen in all African names attributed to God, the latter-God- alone is full actuality and infinite. Other beings, spiritual or otherwise are finite and limited. In African metaphysics, "beings" thus form an intricate nexus of reality. Reality is seen both particularistically and universalistically. But of ultimate importance to the Africans is how things (beings) are holistically interconnected among themselves and with the forces. There is therefore a strong belief in African metaphysics that the "beings" at the top of the hierarchy, the superior beings, can influence or affect, either positively or negatively, the lives of other "beings" such as man, animals and plants at the bottom; hence the doctrine of causality in the African metaphysics. Thus anything that happens either to man or simply in the cosmos has a cause. But man being part of the realm of existence yet only him can be both an object and subject of study at the same time; we have all good reasons to examine him further and in greater detail. In the next section we therefore consider the concept of person in African metaphysics which is confusingly used interchangeably with the concept of Man in ordinary language.

The Conception of Person in African Metaphysics

The African traditional conception of a person is somehow different, though not in totality, from that of the western thought. This denotes that there are a number of differences and similarities of the conceptions of the person found in African traditional thought and western metaphysics.

Generally speaking, African conceptions of person are multifaceted and contain several intrinsic characteristics[7]: 1) a person is made up of numerous components, 2) a person has an active moral component; and that 3) the components are synchronized between the physical and metaphysical bodies. This complexity described in the Bantu-African word for person, muntu (munhu in Shona) is a set of concrete social relationships and a system of systems. Fu-Kiau rightly remarks that: Muntu is "n'kingu a n'kingu" - a principle of principles; such that muntu is able to produce materially or technologically other mechanical systems[8]. This understanding of muntu connotes that a muntu is distinguished from other "beings" found in the realm of existence by intelligence and a unique quality of humanness, besides the physical body that makes distinguishable from other "beings". In so far as a muntu has a dual force vitale/soul-mind, mweya-njere (in Shona dichotomy), which can remain interacting with the local or world community after death (of the body), a muntu can never be comparable to an animal or to a plant.

That said, it is still worth should be noted however that though the African conception of person are multifaceted, as far as Africans are concerned, a person is generally understood as a composite of body (material) and spirit (immaterial) yielding a dualistic conception of the human being, that which we are calling a person. Indeed, the composite and transcendent person is found throughout Africa. In ancient Egypt, for example, the physical body is called the zed or khet and the soul or ba which according to Diop[9] is equivalent of the double of the body found throughout Black Africa, the ka is the immortal soul, or aspect of the divine that is within, the shadow (šwt), the name (ren), and heart (ib). Egyptian cosmology teaches that the ba of the deceased is free to wander, but must return to the body before the sun sets. This metaphysical understanding is shared by many African ethnic groups. For the Zulu of South Africa, for instance, a person is a cluster including the body, aura, Law, and uqobo or essence[10]. And for the Shona of Mozambique and Zimbabwe, a person comprises the physical body or muviri/mutumbi, the soul or mweya which is the divine force within the muviri, the shadow or bvuri and the mind or njere/pfungwa. It is believed in the Shona metaphysics that the bvuri and the njere can be manipulated by witches and where the latter is affected the victim becomes mentally unstable (munhu anobva apenga). Where the bvuri is manipulated by a witch, the victim runs the risk of getting a very bad luck and can be labelled a witch even if s/he is truly not one. Similar is the Nupe's characterization of a person which according to Nadel Frederick[11] includes the body or naka, the soul or rayi, the shadow soul or fifingi, and the personal soul or kuci. Frederick confirms that the fifingi like the bvuri and njere (in Shona cosmology) are vulnerable to external forces, such as witchcraft. In their concept of a person, the Yoruba[12] also include a shadow called the ojiji, the iye or mental body, and oka or heart-soul. Generally speaking, however, the Yoruba concept of person has four main components: ara the physical body, emí, the soul, the orí, or inner head or divinity called the orí, which each person selects before birth, and the esè which is individual effort. The orí determines a person's potential for material success and actualization more so than a predetermined destiny. As a personal divinity, the orí must grant permission before an orisha can bless the person. Your orí is a "free will" choice before birth. Though, once born, it is esè, the individual struggle and strife that determines what potential of the orí will manifest. Whatever personal or functional goal a person has in life, being of good aptitude or moral character, ìwàpele is paramount. Thus the African conception of person is generally the same though the terms used to describe it differ depending on the language in each society.

The African conception of person explicated above is different from western conception of a person which tends to "abstract this or that feature of the lone individual and then proceeds to make it the defining or essential characteristic which entities aspiring to the description 'man' must have"[13]. Thus while the African view of person denies that persons can be defined by focusing on this or that physical or psychological isolated static quality of rationality, will or memory of an individual, the western view of a person confirms this. In African metaphysics, the person is a part of creation like animals, trees, and nature but distinct through empowerment by choice and the ability to consciously direct the energies flowing through all creation. This is to say, generally speaking, African ontology puts the person at the center[14]. A person is different from things, the latter of which cannot raise questions about their beingness and other beings; a person is the cornerstone of the universe and the fullest expression of creation yet is understood through other persons, not abstractly by himself as conceded in Western metaphysics.

Yet there is an important conception of person that both African metaphysics and western metaphysics totally agree. This is the understanding of a person as a moral being. Africans just like westerners believe that only human beings are moral beings. The Yoruba concept of ìwàpele cited above, for example, describes the active moral component of the African person. It distinguishes the muntu (person/human being) from the kintu (thing). In Shona, the concept of unhu (humanness) distinguishes a complete human being (munhu chaiye) from one who is not, a dog like person (haasi munhu, imbwa yemunhu). In other words, a person without morals is not considered a person in the full sense and can never be highly regarded, no matter how big, rich or powerful s/he might be. This is because in Shona, munhu chaiye (a real person) is one who is morally good. This is contrasted with the expressions; haasi munhu (is not a person) or imbwa yemunhu (is a dog mannered person).

Good character is the prerequisite of all human activity in African conduct, including the creation and application knowledge. N'Sengha[15] calls this concept the "thinking heart". He notes that in most Bantu languages, the word "heart" also stands for "thought" and a muntu wa mucima muyampe (a person is not only a person with a good heart in the sense of being kind, compassionate, and generous but also a person of good thought). Thus generally speaking, rationality and morality go hand in glove in the African thought. This concurs with western thought, particularly Socrates/Plato who believed that he who knows the right can never do wrong unless he wills to do so.

The last characteristic of the African person we are going to discuss under this section is the intricate relationship amid the various physical, communal and spiritual components. A person is a person through others (in Shona, munhu munhu kubudikidza navamwe). This understanding, though variously expressed through proverbs, idioms, songs, folktales, among other mediums is widespread in African cosmology. The African concept of person emphasizes much the issue of collectivity or communalism, it concedes indigenous wisdom understands that individual activities impact the entire community. It concedes that each individual is unique. The Zulu Personal Declaration, for example, states that:

My neighbour and I have the same origins;
We have the same life-experience and a common destiny;

My neighbour's sorrow is my sorrow;
His joy is my joy; His survival is a precondition of my survival.
And yet I do not prescribe destiny for my neighbour;
My neighbour is myself in a different guise;
Equals do not prescribe destiny for each other...[16]

The Shona of Mozambique and Zimbabwe being part of African society hold the same view of person. They believe that every member of the society is useful. They capture this philosophy in their idioms like Kuwanda kwakanaka, kwakarambwa nemuroyi (the more we are the better, only a witch is against being many) and Munhu munhu (a person is a person, viz no one should look down upon others). In fact, everyone whether poor or rich, small or big, physically challenged or otherwise has a duty of service (to make the world a better place to live). This philosophy of life by the Zulu and the Shona among other African ethnic groups has been captured though implicitly by scholars like John Mbiti. Mbiti in his famous dictum had this to say: I am because we are, we are therefore I am[17]. The dictum implies that personhood in the African cosmology is defined with reference to the environing community; it is the community which defines the person as a person not the person himself/herself. And in this relation, the reality of the communal world takes precedence over the reality of individual life histories. This is, however, not to say that man is not free to make choice. He can do so but this should not violate the freedom of other community members, otherwise the individual risks suffering sanctions from the community as a whole. Putting it differently, a person in African cosmology, only becomes a person after a process of incorporation and conformity, failure of which would result in the person not fully considered as a person, but a mere person. As explained earlier in this section, a person who fails to conform and achieves the process of incorporation, in Shona society for example, fails to become a full person (haazi munhu: is not a person).This connotes that African conception of person is highly linked to morality. What causes a person considered a person in African thought system is morality (his ability to distinguish the right from the wrong), besides other characteristics discussed above. If a person is considered a person because of some causes or effects, this raises our curiosity to discuss the concept of causality in African metaphysics.

Causality and the Two Worlds of Africa

In African metaphysics, the concept of causality is a very central issue. As previously highlighted the African metaphysical life is permeated by the understanding that nothing happens without a cause – the doctrine of causation. Causation can be defined as making something happen, allowing or enabling something to happen or preventing something from happening[18]. Causation in African metaphysics (as in western metaphysics) is predicated on the maxim that there is no effect without a cause and no action or reality may bring itself into being/existence. The notion of causality is therefore crucial to all African forms of life. This connotes that African cultures appreciate the notion of causality very well just as sciences put it. However, causes of mishaps that befall humanity in the African world-view is generally understood in terms of mystical powers as the agentive causes of such mishaps while western understanding of causality seems to be inclined towards purely scientific or empirical explanations. This is correctly captured by Kwame Gyekye. For Gyekye ,and indeed so, even though Africans are aware of these purely scientific causal explanations, they do not often consider them as profound enough to offer complete satisfaction in accounting for the events of life that they feel need an explanation[19]. The question that is commonly asked is: "Why must a particular event happen to a particular person, at a particular place and in a given time?" This means that the concept of chance is not welcome in African metaphysics as it may have in western metaphysics. In fact, chance does not have a place whatsoever in African Metaphysics. What African metaphysics would call chance is the human ignorance of the series of actions and reactions that have given rise to a given event. But does this mean to say that the African man's world is deterministically ordered through and through such that s/he is not free to make decision in all circumstances?

In view of the question raised, it can be articulated that the African cause and effect nexus still permits the exercise of free-will. Man is free to make decisions and choices. When faced with alternative options, he is free to choose to carry out one or the other. However, in certain cases, the individual may find himself compelled by circumstances beyond his/her control to choose one of the alternative options. In addition, I can say that chance, determinism and freewill when properly understood can be seen as different sides of the same coin. What is considered as chance is what happens accidentally but yet traceable to a cause and a reason. Similarly, what we consider to be a determined event is the aftermath of a freely committed act which has consequently led to a determined cause and effect. It is like free will is opening the door of actions and then determinism takes its turn. This connotes that man as a being is free to some extent and yet limited by his community. Thus in African metaphysics, reality scheme is said to be both individualistic and communitarian or rather collective. Through personal initiative, the individual can exercise his freedom without coming into conflict with the "collective will" of the community to which s/he is part. However, man is free to go against the wishes of the community, but such freedom is always accompanied with sanctions from the community as a whole.

As can be inferred from the discussion above, African metaphysics does not regard the Humean gynaecological intricacies of necessary conditions for causality such as priority in time, constant conjunction, necessary connection, and contiguity in time and space. Neither do the Africans bother themselves about the Cartesian problem of interactionism (of the mind and the body). It seems due to lack of serious and rigorous metaphysical inquiry by African metaphysicians it is even taken for granted that the body and the spirit though having different natures interact through forces as explained in this chapter. Perhaps, having noted this reluctance in African metaphysicians Godwin Sogolo rightly observed:

> One of the puzzles that face those seeking to understand traditional African belief system is how, in the explanation of observable events, disembodied or non-extended entities

(spirits), witches, ghosts, gods, etc. Existing beyond the confines of space could possibly be invoked as causes. This problem arises mainly due to the widespread mechanistic view of causality where - - - necessary connection is assumed to exist between the cause and effect, along Humean argument[20].

The position maintained by Sogolo is that the conception of causality today is so loose and varied in meaning. For this reason Sogolo rightly argues that:

What counts as a causal explanation of an event would depend on factors such as the nature of the event to be explained, our interest in the event, whether the event has one cause or a multiplicity of necessary causes, whether, when the causes are more than one, they can be compatibly invoked and finally whether some of the causes are sufficient such that the others are unnecessary and superfluous[21].

It is clear from Sogolo's argument that there are different conceptions that could constitute causal explanation. These conceptions are numerous especially in Western metaphysics. I am, however, not going to venture into such varied conceptions like Aristotle's material, formal, efficient and final causes which try to explain causality in all cases. My project here is only is to demonstrate how causality is understood in African metaphysics. Until contemporary times mystical thinking has remained central in African metaphysics as in African cosmology in general. For this reason, African metaphysics looks at cause and effect from the point of view of imaginable range of possibilities which include oracles for the final verdict. This thinking is clearly manifested in African metaphysics when people try to explain cases of mishaps, illness and death. Such events are significant for Africans and do not occur without reason or cause. The cause if carefully investigated can be determined. Here beliefs about the nature and operation of causal agents thus cease to be theoretical but must serve as the basis for practical remedial action. Significant events do not occur without reason and the cause can be determined if one investigates carefully. To aid investigations, a traditional healer is normally consulted. This is because a traditional healer is regarded as a panacea to this inquiry since s/he has the capacity to dialogue with the spiritual world in order to explain that which afflict those in this mundane world. The causes most frequently cited to explain serious cases of misfortune and illness and to account for death are the operations of witchcraft or sorcery and punishment by the ancestral spirits which are believed to reside in the "world beyond"; hence Africa's two worlds – the visible/physical world and the world beyond/spiritual world – are separated but interconnected. To keep check on misfortunes, illnesses and inexplicable deaths, the ancestral spirits hold their descendants and successors responsible for the proper conduct of lineage affairs, maintenance of the customs they established and proffering the ritual attention they require. This has negatively affected Africans (African metaphysicians included) to the extent that they give up on the search for empirical causal explanations of causal relations between natural phenomena/events as they resort to supernatural causation. The Africans have found it very difficult to disentangle themselves from the world beyond given the close connection between the people in the physical world with their ancestors in the world beyond. And for them what distinguishes and separates those in the mundane world from those in the world beyond is not only their body constituents but passage of time; hence the need for us to examine the African concept of time.

The Conception of Time in African Metaphysical Discourse

Defining time in African communities can be seen as an aspect of spatial history. It is an attempt to reshape, redefine and redirect postcolonial discourses in ways that are appropriate for the communities that are subjects of those discourses. This work as postcolonial literature is one among those with the aim to deconstruct and "decentre" imperial literature establishing a different agenda and enabling local communities to create their own centres[22]. In this context exploring the way other African cultures conceive time can be seen as part of the effort to shift from the imperial centre to the others – centres in postcolonial African discourses – which were once demonized and marginalized. This is done in a bid to rediscover and re-write the "lost" African self-awareness, thus re-claiming African philosophies and cultural identities in its fullest.

The concept of time is common place in African culture, and so in African metaphysics. It is, however, called differently due to differences in languages across the continent. For example, the Zulu (South Africa), Shangana (Mozambique), Shona (Zimbabwe) word for time is isikati, nkama and nguva respectively.

The concept of time in Africa, like any philosophical term, is confusing and multifaceted. It addresses a plethora of phenomenal aspects of life ranging from agriculture, astronomy, genealogy, ecology, and economic cycles among others. Just like in Western metaphysics, time is conceived fundamentally important in African metaphysics. This is rightly captured by John Mbiti who on talking of time in African sense had it that "time is the key to our understanding of the basic religious and philosophical concepts and may help explain practices and general way of life of African peoples not only in the traditional set up but also in the modern situation"[23]. However, it should be remarked that time in African cosmology is meaningful at the point of the event and not at the mathematical moment. For this reason, schedules and deadlines are not binding in African cultures as may be the case in western cultures. In the past cultures, relationships are more important. Time is not some impersonal entity that can be detached from human relationships like in monochromic societies (western cultures) where schedules and deadlines take precedence over human relationships. Among the Bantu-Congo, for instance, abstract time exists but "it is danga (events) that make time perceptible, providing the unending flow of time with specific 'dams,' events, or 'periods of time."[24] This understanding is pervasive among other Bantu speaking people. They all consider time to be cyclical. A day, for example, falls and starts where it started yesterday. The image that expresses African time thus is the cosmogramic altar or dikeng (in Congo). The circumference of the circle is time and the four points are n'kama as they represent events that take place in each of the points. This image can represent time on a cosmic, a natural, or a human scale. This understanding is premised from the fact that people, animals, inventions and social systems are all conceived and lives through four stages: pregnancy, birth, maturity, and death. In Shona, this conception of time, notwithstanding the Shonas' understanding that history repeats itself, is expressed in their common saying: Chimwe nechimwe chine nguva yacho (everything has its own time). On a natural scale, a year, for instance is divided into parts depending on events that take place during particular moment of the year. The Shonas' year, for example, is divided into mwaka (seasons) such as zhizha (rain season), chirimo (winter). These can further be sub-divided again and again depending on various other events common in these seasons. The names of their months which are time symbolic depict all events that repeatedly take place all year round (depending on time of the year). The months of Nyamavhuvhu (lit windy-August), Gumiguru (lit the tenth month-October) and Mbudzi (lit goat-November), for example, all depict the time of the year when it is too windy, the tenth month of the year and the time when goats normally have kids. Similarly, the Tsonga people of Mozambique call the summer and winter seasons, malanga and uxika respectively. Like what we have seen above on discussion about the Shona, the Tsonga subdivide the seasons into various parts depending on events of the particular moments of the time. Malanga can be sub-divided into nkama (time slots) i.e. nkama wa ukanyu (time for fruit brewed beer). And the Xhosa[25] (of South Africa) have names such as Eyomqungu — for January, which is the month of tall grass and February is EyomDumba which is the month of swelling when the grains fill up. Thus generally African names for all months of the year are time symbolic as they depict events (natural or otherwise) that commonly recur (each year) right round the year. This conception of time is not peculiar to the ethnic groups discussed above, but to Africa as a whole. The idea that African time is divided into parts has been captured in philosophy literature by John Mbiti. Mbiti[26] proposes African time as consisting of two dimensions: sasa and zamani. Sasa, a Kiswahili word meaning now or at present includes events that are about to occur, occurring, or recently experienced. It is where people are conscience of existence or where their perception of existence is focused. Sasa has its own past, present, and future, though narrowly defined. The future would be events that are part of the rhythm of natural phenomena, and other events would be "no-time". Sasa is unique, relative to the individual and reflective of his or her experiences. The community sasa is bigger than the individual's and equally focused on the "nowness of experience". Mbiti's second category, Zamani, consists of "big time" and means ancient times, antiquity, epoch, already, earlier, and before in Kiswahili. Zamani has its own past present and future. Zamani is where the myths that support the cosmology of a community exist. It is the home of people who died long ago and the future home of individuals who physically die and are no longer remembered. It is the period beyond which nothing can go – the final storehouse for all phenomenon and events – and, a reality that is not after or before. Because zamani houses the collective myth of a people by which they live, it supports sasa. It gives foundation to the rituals, dances, and experiences of now. And in turn, as an individual collects experiences, physically dies and is no longer remembered, they move into a nourish zamani. Mbiti, however, has been criticized by scholars such as Kwasi Wiredu for his assertion that an African perception of time is two dimensional so it cannot contain a future, particularly in the context of philosophy.

Perhaps one more aspect of African time important to adumbrate is the African cosmogram. Among the Africans, the cornerstone of the cosmogram is the beginning. The Bantu-Shona call this mavambo, the Shangana; kusungula ka misava; the Zulu, uku cala kwe muhlaba; and Bantu-Congo, musoni. Though words for beginning among Africans differ depending on the language of each culture, it generally points to the same thing- the beginning. The beginning, Africa-wise, refers to the creation of the universe, a time of the sparkle of the on-going process of time and life [27]and formation of the physical earth and all that is in it. For nature, it is the time when a seed is put into the ground, the time of human conception in the womb, and the time an idea takes form in the mind. It can also mean the time of the sun rising, and the physical birth of a person. All this explicates what has already alluded to-that time in African cosmology is explained through events. Koné[28] confirms this conception of time, but making reference to the Mali people. He remarks that among the people of Mali, time has an ecological, ritual, and genealogical context. This is generally the same in all African cultures. The ecological context is based on a conceptual cycle of events that constitute the passage of seasons. These events are composed of pragmatic choices that are performed based on natural phenomena or when they will be successful, not necessarily a specific mathematical time. A good example is the Dogon[29] (of Egypt) circumcision ritual that is postponed if by midsummer Sirius does not shine according to expectations. Therefore, the fact that an event sometimes serves as temporal orientation does not mean that the times when they occur are ritual or religious times to which people are bound – the times can change depending on circumstances. Similarly, genealogical time depends more on context (like space and place) than on precise chronology. Koné[30] further gives an example of the Mande and explains: Among the Mande, we relate to space by talking about events (evidence), while Westerners refer to events by mentioning time (abstract).

While the African conception of time constitutes a number of profound and interesting metaphysical issues, time and space limit me to pursue the subject any further. Suffice to assert that despite the mind boggling puzzles and small variations across African cultures, Africans share the general metaphysical view that time is cyclic and symbolic. That granted I can only record my conviction that African metaphysics is a discipline whose legitimacy is equal to any other field of inquiry studied in colleges and universities today.

Notes

1. John Locke cited in William R. Carter. The Elements of Metaphysics, Temple University Press: USA, 1989, pp. 3.
2. William R. Carter. Ibid. pp.51-52.
3. Ralph M. McInerny. The Logic of Analogy. The Hague: Martinus Nijhoff., 1961, .pp.2.
4. Opoku, Asare, West African Traditional Religion Accra: FEP International Private Ltd, 1978.pp.9-10

5. Richard A. Wright (Ed). African Philosophy, An Introduction. 3rd Ed. University Press of America: New York, 2000, pp.35.
6. Opoku, Asare, West African Traditional Religion Accra: FEP International Private Ltd., 1978.pp.35.
7. Kaphagawani, Didier Njirayamanda. "African Conceptions of a Person: A Critical Survey" Companion to African Philosophy. Ed. Kwasi Wiredu. Malden, MA: Blackwell Publishing, 2004. Pp.332-342.
8. Fu-Kiau, Kimbwandende Kia Bunseki. African Cosmology of the Bantu-Kongo Tying the Spiritual Knot Principles of Life and Living, Brooklyn, NY: Athelia Henrietta Press, 2001.pp.42.
9. Diop, Cheikh Anta. Civilization or Barbarism: An Authentic Anthropology. (Eds). H.J. Salemson and M. de Jager. Translated by Yaa-Lengi Meema Ngemi. Chicago: Lawrence Hill, 1991.
10. Molefi Kete Asante and Abu S Abarry. "Zulu Personal Declaration" in African Intellectual Heritage. Philadelphia: Temple University Press, 1996, pp. 371-378.
11. Nadel, Siegfried Frederick. Nupe Religion. London: Routledge & Kegan Paul, 1954.
12. Abímbolá, Kolá. Yorùbá Culture: A Philosophical Account. Birmingham, UK: Ìrókò Academic Publishers, 2006.
13. Ifeanyi A. Menkiti. "Person and community in African traditional thought" in Richard A. Wright (Ed). African Philosophy, An Introduction. 3rd Ed. University Press of America: New York, 2000, pp.171.
14. Mbiti, John S. African Religions and Philosophy, 2d ed. Oxford: Heinemann, 1990.pp.145.
15. Nkulu-N'Sengha, M. "African Epistemology" Encyclopedia of Black Studies. Eds. Molefi Asante and Ama Mazama. Thousand Oaks, CA: Sage, 2005.p.42.
16. Molefi Kete Asante and Abu S Abarry. "Zulu Personal Declaration" in African Intellectual Heritage. Philadelphia: Temple University Press, 1996, pp.372
17. Mbiti, John S. Op.cit.pp.145.
18. Sanford, D.H. 1975, "The direction of causation and the direction of conditionship," Journal of Philosophy vol.73, pp.193
19. Gyekye, Kwame. African Cultural Values. Philadelphia: Sankofa Publishing Company, 1996, pp.28.

20. Sogolo, Godwin, Foundations of African Philosophy. Ibadan, Ibadan University Press, 1993.pp. 103-104.
21. Sogolo, Godwin, Ibid, 1993, pp.104.
22. Ngugi WA Thiong'o. Writers in Politics. Oxford: James Currey. 1997.
23 Mbiti, John S. Op cit. pp. 19.
24. Fu-Kiau, K.K. Bunseki. "Ntangu-Tandu-Kolo: The Bantu-Kongo Concepts of Time," Time in the Black Experience. Ed. Joseph Adjaye. Westport, CT: Greenwood Press, 1994.pp20.
25. Neethling, Siebert, Jacob, Black Elk Speaks: Native American (Indian) Onomastics. Nomina Africana. 7:1 & 2: 1993. 17-36.
26 Mbiti, John S. Op. cit. pp.22.
27. Fu-Kiau, K.K. Bunseki. Op cit. pp.23.
28. Koné, Kassim. "Time and Culture among the Bamana/Mandinka and Dogon of Mali." Time in the Black Experience. Ed. Joseph Adjaye. Westport, CT: Greenwood Press. 1994, pp.91.
29. Koné, Kassim, Ibid.pp.91.
30. Koné, Kassim, Ibid.pp.93.

Chapter Four

The Nexus between African Metaphysics and Indigenous Epistemologies

In chapter two African metaphysics has been defined as a branch of philosophy that systematically investigates causes and the nature of ultimate reality from an African perspective. It deals with first principles and seeks to explain the nature of "being" or reality (ontology) and the origin and structure of the universe (cosmology) as understood from an African view point. I will add one more point here: that African metaphysics is closely associated with African epistemology (as metaphysics in general is closely associated with epistemology). Given this relationship, it becomes necessary for us to look at the nexus between African metaphysics and African indigenous epistemology.

Research on ancient African civilization suggests that Africans perceived the world differently from the world view imposed on them by European colonialists. The latter's influence resulted in some western scholars mentioned earlier in this book – Hume, Kant and Hegel – to deny reason to the people of other societies like Africa. By denying reason to Africa, they were also denying epistemology and other critical forms of knowledge to Africans. I will, however, quickly say they were mistaken. Unlike western philosophy which emphasizes individualism, a strong interpersonal relationship with others as well as harmony, peace with nature, communalism, and spirituality have always characterized African philosophies, and specifically African epistemology and African metaphysics. There is ample evidence pointing to that African epistemology dates as far back as 4000 B.C.E. This include three scripts of ancient Egypt: hieroglyphic, hieratic, and demotic; Meroitic and Coptic scripts of Nubia; Sabean and G'eez scripts of Ethiopia; the Toma and Vai scripts of Liberia; and the Mum script of Cameroon[1] among other evidence. A strong emphasis was however placed on the Egyptian scripts and history because Afrocentric scholars concluded that the greatest world achievements have come out of Egyptian civilization. This means that although much of

African history had been passed down by oral traditions, these scripts gave clues to ancient African indigenous epistemologies and metaphysics. It is an undeniable appreciation, therefore, that as early as 4000 B.C.E., some Africans – the Egyptians for example – had already established not only an epistemological system, but also a spiritual system of metaphysics, law, order, truth, and morality to guide them. This is so because African epistemology placed and indeed still places great emphasis on metaphysics, ethics/morality, spirituality, symbolism, mystical science, customs and tradition. Since time immemorial the African world view, thus, was understood and interpreted through a spiritual source among other sources – the reason why there is a strong nexus between African metaphysics and African epistemology. No reality existed without a mystical or spiritual inclination. The universe, nature, humans, knowledge and the spirit were all considered one.

African epistemology is interpreted through traditional customs and practices which in themselves emphasize the close connections between the empirical world and the cosmos. Parallels can be drawn between the consequences of good and bad, given that the African cosmological world – vadzimu and musikavanhu (ancestors and God/ the creator, respectively)- is believed to govern the empirical world, and in consequence, judges humanity according to the virtue of their deeds. The cosmovision of the African people is based on three worlds: the human world, the spiritual world and the natural world[2]. In this trio relation, the spirit mediums act as intermediaries between mortal beings and the "living dead" or ancestral spirits. Transcending this view, I argue that indigenous knowledge systems (IKSs) heretofore used interchangeably with African epistemologies are the adhesive vice grips that links the cosmological world with the spirit mediums, rainmakers, and rural dwellers' social relations and bind them together by setting the ground rules in terms of cultural practices and customs observance in their communities. These epistemologies are used, for example, in the processions of traditional ceremonies such as rain-making and witch-naming to mention but a few. In light of the coordination or facilitation roles in spiritual activities that IKSs perform, the latter should be conceived as a spiritual commitment of the "land dwellers" to the ancestors of the land through allegiance to the traditions, values, customs and metaphysical beliefs held and known through the knowledge systems. Now that we have discussed, though briefly, the connection between African metaphysics and indigenous epistemology we turn on to a detailed discussion on IKS as African epistemology. We will revisit the discussion on the nexus between African epistemology and African metaphysics towards the end of this chapter.

Indigenous Knowledge System as African Epistemology

Since time immemorial indigenous knowledge systems (IKSs) were used by societies in Africa and other parts of the world for various purposes depending on the needs of the society in question. IKSs, thus, have survived on for a very long time. But, what are IKSs?

IKSs can be defined as local knowledge(s) that is unique to a given culture or society[3]. They are knowledge forms that have failed to die despite the racial and colonial onslaughts that they have suffered at the hands of western imperialism and arrogance[4]. It is important to emphasize that IKSs as forms of knowledge have originated locally and naturally. Considering the sense of the two definitions given above, my conception of IKSs identifies with Ocholla who perceives IKS as a complex set of knowledge and technologies existing and developed around specific conditions of populations and communities indigenous to a particular geographic area[5]. The complexity of IKS results from the logical qualification with the word "system" as it suggests a network of processes with different components, such as knowledge, belief and technology. On the other hand, IKSs are "indigenous" because the meanings as well as the categories of sense making are generated internally within a cultural community and are/were produced through "indigenous" thinking or exploration whether material, philosophical or linguistic. This means indigenous knowledge can also be understood (if you like) as local knowledge, local technical knowledge, indigenous ecological knowledge, community knowledge and in some cases, even folkloric knowledge. What commonly underlies all these bodies is the fact that they are developed through the processes of acculturation and through kinship relationships that societal groups form, and are handed down to the posterity through oral tradition as well as cultural practices like rituals and rites. As such, IKS are the adhesives that bind society as they constitute communicative processes through which knowledge is transmitted, preserved and acquired by humans in a given society. It should be emphasized that in IKS certain elements from other cultures may be assimilated over time. This knowledge is considered indigenous despite being contemporary. Indigenous knowledge need not essentially be traditional in nature. Contemporary knowledge serving indigenous ends, or using indigenous materials or processed through indigenous rules or heuristics can also be part of IKSs provided it is interpreted through local cultural meanings. A fine example is India's knowledge of tea growing and making. Until two hundred years ago, India did not cultivate tea bushes. Today, India is one of the biggest consumers of tea. Lot of indigenous knowledge has evolved around the tea plants, tea making and using the waste and used tea leaves.

As noted earlier in this book, Africa has an old and rich philosophy. Its IKSs which are a unique genre of epistemology is a good example of Africa's treasure. These include: runyoka (fencing a woman/man with charm), rukwa (fencing property with charm) and zvierwa (taboos). Another controversial example is ngozi (avenging spirits). Because all these are transmitted through cultural rites (for example, rituals), through socialisation processes and can be appropriated through kinship ties, they qualify as IKSs. These IKSs are commonplace in many African societies across Africa.

It can be further elaborated that IKSs are linked to the communities that produce them. For this reason, they are better understood by the members of the community from which the IKSs were developed than any other people. More important is the observation that those knowledge systems are characterized by complex kinship systems of relationships among people, animals, the earth and the cosmos from which knowing emanates. For this reason IKSs are known by other names, and among them are indigenous ways of knowing, traditional knowledge, indigenous technical knowledge, rural knowledge as well as ethno-science or indigenous people's science[6]. And, they manifest themselves through different dimensions. Among these are agriculture, medicine, security, botany, zoology, craft skills and linguistics. In matters relating to security, especially of properties like homes, field crops and livestock, the indigenous people of Africa developed some mechanisms that are still, instead of security guards/police, used in many rural areas to safeguard their properties from thieves and invaders. They have also developed traditional ways of weather forecasting that helped them to plan their activities for at least two to three days in advance. Since time immemorial this knowledge was very useful especially in summer and immediately after harvesting when crops like finger millet would be in need of thrashing and winnowing. Indigenous ways of knowing have also brought forth useful knowledge on medicine and health. The use of proverbs and idioms is another case of ethno-knowledge that has been used, for example, in both judicial and governance matters.

It is curious to note that IKSs as those forms of knowledge that the people of the formerly colonized countries survived on before the advent of colonialism were swept aside and demonized by the colonialists as unempirical and superstitious science. This was chiefly because the colonialists sought to give themselves some form of justification on why they had to colonize other people's lands. As they colonized others, they did not only subject the indigenous people to inhuman treatment. They also took away their lands and renamed these using names from the metropolis, and added insult to injury by claiming that the indigenous people were in the dark and were backward such that their indigenous knowledge and philosophies were nothing but myths. This is underscored in the works of scholars such as David Hume, Immanuel Kant and Hegel who surprisingly denied reason, the most essential quality of humanity, to other groups of people[7] like those Africans. All that was African was therefore looked down upon. This consequently resulted to what I call "fallacy of science". We will look at this in some details in the next section.

African Epistemology and the Fallacy of Science

African epistemology is deeply connected to the African beliefs, particularly beliefs in the spiritual world-the world beyond-and life in disembodied forms (lives believed to reside in the world beyond). This is to say the belief in life in disembodied bodies and in the world beyond is considered by Africans to be the sources of inspiration – the springboard-for the African epistemologies.

The puzzle of how the immaterial spiritual entities come to interact and continue to influence the activities of the living, thus, does not arise for the Africans as it does for those who subscribe to the mechanistic view of the world. Yet the ideas of life in disembodied forms and the world beyond are not difficult to understand once one has understood the fact that the Africans in their metaphysical and epistemological world views include a belief in immortality of the soul (the spiritual part of human being) and in the "world beyond". Traditionally, Africans believe in the existence of spiritual entities. Spiritual beings are very much counted among the living as important participants in shaping everything that may happen and by their very nature they now occupy a better position in determining events and influencing them, as they are no longer subject to the limitations of space and time. These entities are many in the African cosmology and are believed to be the sources for most of the Africans' epistemological beliefs, yet expert science has always been adamant to recognize them as real sources of knowledge. This has mainly been due to the so-called scientism and what we shall call "fallacy of science". I will discuss these in some detail in the next few pages.

Though Africans themselves never had difficulties in unpacking the metaphysical and epistemological relationships between the living and the world beyond (the spiritual world) the problem appeared with the advent of colonialism alongside its scientism in Africa. With scientism and its emphasis on empiricism, the barriers to unravelling the relationship between the living and the world beyond were inevitable, yet let alone resulting in science committing the so-called "fallacy of science". Fallacy of science is "science's inability to provide scientific explanations to issues of metaphysical nature and to present alternative convincing explanations outside the canonical frameworks of scientific inquiry"[8]. While science seeks to offer powerful, convincing explanations about diverse issues of nature notwithstanding its limitations, some civil unrest in western world contexts have been instigated by the same scientific studies that have proven to be faulty, or inconclusive, and the public has instigated independent inquiries to invalidate scientific findings of experts. Durant cites Beck who suggests that the "scientisation"[9] of protest against science means that even to dispute the scientific position of an opponent one usually relies upon science to make a persuasive challenge. This has been the dilemma of science when confronted with issues of metaphysical nature like "life in disembodied form and the world beyond" where recourse to scientific laws and methods has proven to offer limited results. The providence of science in explaining phenomena owes itself to its internal logic, perceived objectivity and power of prediction that may not immediately apply to metaphysical beliefs like life in disembodied form and world beyond. As Harding[10] suggests, most of the greatest successes of science owe to its "internal logic" be it as inductivism, crucial experiments, the hypothetico-deductive method, or a cycle of normal science-revolution-normal science. I infer from Harding that the authority of science rest upon its objective claims and its ability to render scientific proof that is perceivably immune to personal biases, preferences and values. Given the complexity of establishing scientific proof about the existence of life in disembodied bodies and the world beyond, it is surprising how the subject of disembodied bodies has not attracted the much needed curiosity amongst scientists, but rather left to religion and metaphysicians.

    A complementary view is that beliefs in life in disembodied bodies and in the world beyond rest on internalism, and as such cannot be subjected to scientific rigor. As Ikuenobe[11] notes, internalism suggests that rationality is a function of the properties of beliefs such as coherence to which one has internal access. The belief in disembodied bodies and in the world beyond is internalist in orientation; it invokes some internally coherent claims about explanation of the functioning of the cosmology to which scientific investigation is less privileged to infer from or draw on. The existences of life in disembodied form and in the world beyond are such metaphysical beliefs whose functioning defies recourse to scientific explanation, or prediction to sufficiently and epistemically substantiate their existence. Yet the challenge is that the authority of science and its hegemonic influence on knowledge production has undermined possibilities for other epistemological alternatives for explicating social reality/nature in ways that fall outside the frameworks of science, particularly how life in disembodied form can illuminate one's knowledge of cosmology and what new epistemological insights about the world beyond could be gained from exploration of this metaphysical reality.

The dominance of science and perceptions about its opaqueness to the public have led to a focus on "back-end" consequences such as risk, in effect protecting the broader trajectory of scientific and technological development from accountability[12]. This raises critical questions about whether different forms of knowledge, (for example African epistemology) cannot be developed outside the terms and parameters defined by science. What is lost in the process of moving from conventional scientific inquiry towards the unorthodox processes of searching for other forms of knowing like examining life in disembodied form and making speculations on the world beyond? These questions cannot be adequately addressed without challenging the monopoly of science as the predominant way of accessing, communicating and transmitting knowledge. The rise in "citizen science" participatory processes of public understanding and even challenging of science research is the direct consequence of public frustration with the limitations of science. I should not be mistaken as arguing for abandoning expert science, but rather I seek to warn against the uncritical acceptance of science as neutral and instrumental. I identify with Heidegger who warns that the naive celebration of technology leads to being chained and imprisoned by technology. He cautions that:

> We shall never experience our relationship to the essence of technology so long as we conceive and merely push forward the technological [...] Everywhere we remain unfree and chained to technology, whether we passionately affirm or

deny it [...] But we are delivered to it in the worst possible way as we regard it as something neutral[13].

In line with Heidegger's conceptualization, I argue for the recognition of African processes of searching for other forms of knowing. Belief in life in disembodied form and the world beyond are metaphysical realities that can help people still in their biological/physical bodies to behave themselves in an altruistic manner that could contribute easing the tapestry of Africa's human development and promotion of unity, peace and order. The belief can be a source of "moral knowledge". That is to say, life in disembodied form and the world beyond embody a hidden genre of epistemology or different form of metaphysical knowledge that could contribute in multiple ways to resolving Africa's development dilemmas, if it cast in the open for debate, and integrated into mainstream expert science. I argue that the epistemological exploration of the world beyond and of life in disembodied form are a potentially beneficial indigenous knowledge system that for long, has been conceived as nonsensical and mythical by Western civilisation and whose developmental essence remains shrouded in mystery.

I am inclined to point out that the discussion of the world beyond and life in disembodied lives takes us to another critical question, the question of life after bodily death. As such, I invite my readers to the African conception of life and death, the concepts which I shall refer to as the "persisting link" between African metaphysics and African epistemology. I find these issues worth discussing in the next section because the belief on life and death are central not only to African metaphysics as has been demonstrated in the previous chapters, but also to African epistemology.

The Persisting Link between African Epistemology and African Metaphysics

We have examined the general connection between African metaphysics and epistemology at the beginning of this chapter. We will, however, discuss the subject once again, but using the concepts of "life" and "death". This is to enable us to unveil and understand the persisting link between the two African philosophies (African epistemology and African metaphysics). These concepts are critical in African philosophy in so far as questions about them can lead us to either a discussion on African epistemology or on African metaphysics, depending on how the questions are presented. For example, where questions about the concepts attempt to arrive by rational means at a general picture of the African world view – African reality – the discussion leads us to African metaphysics. And, where the questions attempt to rationally affirm or negate the truth of African beliefs about these concepts, we venture into African epistemology territory. Put differently, the idea of life and death is metaphysical in so far as it concerns issues bordering the extra-mental, spiritual, abstract, universal or the transcendental realities. On the other hand, it is epistemological as it calls for the identification of principles for evaluation of the belief itself to determine its truth. Evaluation of a belief is always done with a particular goal, that is, for us to acquire true justified beliefs that cannot "'fly away'" and avoid false beliefs. That said, we can see that the concepts of life and death are at the borderline of African metaphysics and African epistemology; hence their treatment as the persisting link between African metaphysics and epistemology.

In the light of the analysis above, I feel secure to discuss the concept of "life" and "death" – if you will, a belief in life after bodily death – under the topic on African epistemology.

There is a long tradition in western epistemology that focuses on reasons for our beliefs. We will look at this tradition before our discussion's African belief in life after bodily death. According to the aforementioned tradition, it is not enough that we acquire true beliefs, for example, belief about life and bodily death; we must also have necessary and adequate reasons for thinking that such beliefs are likely to be epistemologically true. The assessment of the adequacy of our reasons for believing is an integral part of the traditional view of epistemology: the view that describes knowledge as a true justified belief. We will use this general characterization of epistemology to examine the belief in life after bodily death as conceived from an African epistemological point of view. This would enable us to determine whether the African belief on life after bodily death is true, justified and not a result of wishful thinking or confused thinking as critics would say. If the traditional African belief of life after bodily death passes this test then it can be said to be epistemically legitimate.

Given the nature of concepts as those being examined – life and death – it needs mentioning that the concepts are deeply controversial and a bit intimidating, for practical as well as philosophical reasons. For this reason, they can be clearly understood if and only if we first look at how they developed and came into use. Here, we shall use the word concept to refer to certain properties that pick out all and only things of a particular kind. In view of this understanding, Aristotle[14] discusses the concept of life in his book de Anima and makes this argument: "plants and animals just like human beings possess a 'psyche'" – a word which is sometimes misleadingly translated as "soul" and sometimes much more appropriately as "life principle". He correctly observes that "what has soul (psyche) differs from what has not in that the former displays life."[15] To this end, three levels of life were identified. These are nutritional/vegetative life (plant life with powers of reproduction), animal life (with powers of sensation including those of the lower levels) and human life (intellectual powers including those of the lower levels). Since human life is at the highest level, it follows that "there is more to life in man than in a dog, in a dog than in a worm, in a worm than in a plant, and in a plant than in a stone"[16]; hence, Aristotle's famous scala naturae: ladder of nature. From the understanding that life is characterized by the "psyche" which thinks, reasons and wills, life has been technically construed as the condition that distinguishes animate things from inanimate things including the capacity for growth, reproduction, functional activity and continual change preceding death. For the present, life shall be considered solely in the light of human beings and not animate "things" in the other two levels mentioned above.

On the other hand, death has been construed as the permanent state of being unconscious[17]. It is admitted in this definition that death is only death if there is permanent inactivity due to complete cessation of life in an animate thing, otherwise, it would be better considered as a temporary state of unconsciousness. Thus, death is in sharp contrast to life which involves consciousness.

In view of the concepts "life" and "death" discussed above, the belief in "life after bodily death" denotes the existence of once bodily animate things, in this case human beings, sometime after cessation of life has taken place. In African cosmology, it can also be understood as "afterlife"[18] since life after bodily death is believed to take place only after some form of life has empirically existed before in a human body which is now dead. Put differently, it is life ensuing death of the human body. We will discuss this belief in a bit of some details here.

So far, the issue of life after bodily death receives different interpretations in philosophical circles. Some people dismiss it wholly as a myth, and amongst the believers are those who believe that life after bodily death is only possible in bodily form and others who believe that it is only possible in disembodied form (non-bodily form). It can be argued that only one and not all these views can be true, and so the different interpretations that the issue of afterlife receives make it a contested notion. This also justifies the need for a rigorous examination of the epistemic legitimacy of the belief. In the Bible, Jesus said that if one wanted to put new wine into old wine skins, one had to first destroy the old ones and put the new wine in the new wine skins, otherwise the wine will burst the skins, and wine is lost and so are the skins. Using the same approach, it is arguably true that in order to establish the African belief in life after bodily death (of human beings) as a reality and/or a myth, there is need to put to rest the existing views to make way for the "new civilization".

African believers in life after bodily death are in two categories; believers in life after death in bodily form and believers in life after death in disembodied form. Let us examine the former before advancing an argument on the later, the category within which most of the African metaphysicians and epistemologists fall.

Starting with the view on life after death in bodily form, western philosophers, particularly the Pythagoreans believed in reincarnation, that is, the taking up of another bodily form by the soul after death. For them, after death, a human being's soul is either demoted or promoted to various forms of animals depending on his or her previous personality[19]. In this case, the soul of a dead human being can transmigrate into the body of a dog or to another human being as a continuation of its mode of life depending on the conduct of the previous life. To this end, two mind-boggling questions can however be asked; if the soul transmigrates into a donkey, for example, would we consider the "being" continuing in this mode of life a donkey or a human being? And, if the soul transmigrates into another human being, would it mean that the human being to whom the soul has transmigrated is now in possession of two souls? Moreover, is it possible for the soul to migrate into another dead body and revive its life? All these questions are pointers to the inadequacies of the Pythagoreans' theory of reincarnation. It is, thus, my contention that the Pythagoreans' epistemological view of life after bodily death is tantamount to chasing the wind. It leaves a lot more unsaid, and so it cannot be epistemologically accepted as a reasonable answer to the question of life after bodily death.

Resurrection theorists, giving what they know of human beings, have also argued for life after bodily death in bodily form. The basis of their argument lies in the Christian religion. It is premised on the belief that Christians ask in Jesus' name and the Bible says that Jesus was crucified by the Jews. The assumption by Christians here is that Jesus did not only die once and for all but resurrected (rose from death in his bodily form) and is still living. The eschatological drama of Jesus (if it is true) would mean that there is life after death in bodily form. What casts epistemological doubt on the theory, however, is that many Christians, perhaps due to fear of the unknown (uncertain of whether they will resurrect as Jesus did), are afraid of bodily death. If they are certain about what they believe, why should they doubt their resurrection? It is through this character in Christians, that critics have found loopholes to argue that the resurrection of Jesus (which is the basis of Christian theorists' argument) is highly questionable as a historical event for the body of Jesus was stolen from the tomb; it did not resurrect. If this argument is epistemically true (as it appears) and the fear for bodily death remains, then, we are bound to doubt any argument (by the Christian theorists) which defends life after bodily death in bodily form.

Having put to rest arguments by those who defend the issue of life after bodily death in bodily form, we will now turn to the African belief of life after bodily death in disembodied form-belief in bodiless persons recognized as human beings. This is the belief African traditional metaphysicians and indigenous epistemology subscribe to. It is the belief that scientists have always despised on the basis of scientism, yet it is a belief that is epistemologically plausible especially from an African view point.

Though the idea of life after bodily death in disembodied form is very old in African epistemology, its main historical thrust for us today comes from one of Plato's dialogues, the Phaedo. This has chiefly been due to lack of the writing tradition in Africa. In the dialogue, Socrates' defence of the belief in life after death begins with the question: Does a man's soul ceases to exist when he has died?[20] Here, in the Phaedo, Socrates is presented as having been condemned to death by Melotos, Anytos and Lycon, accused of impiety and of corrupting the youth. His lifelong friends, Criton, Semmias the Theban and Cebes, among others, are grief-stricken and even persuade Socrates to seek asylum in a foreign land, Thessaly. Criton, for instance, had this to say to Socrates: "if you like to go to Thessaly I have friends there who will make much of you safe so that no one in Thessaly shall hurt you. I do not think you are undertaking a right thing by throwing yourself away when you can be free."[21] Though there was room for him to escape bodily death, Socrates assured his friends that he was perfectly capable of surviving death for his death was simply a transition from this world to some happier state of the blessed: the "world beyond". In his words, "death will be a wonderful blessing, a migration of soul from this world to another place."[22] In this passage, Socrates rightly distinguished between himself (soul) and his body. He thought of his real self as something distinct from his body- something that survives the death of the body.

In the 'modern' era, Socrates' view has gained wide acceptance and veneration through the metaphysical and epistemological works of Rene Descartes and Richard Swinburne. In his Meditations on first Philosophy, Descartes rightly contends that he is a thinking thing. Of course, he can doubt that he has a body but he cannot doubt that he exists for nothing can doubt unless it is something. For this reason, Descartes is pretty certain that his "self" is distinct from his body and can surely exist without it. He says in the second Meditation, "I can doubt that my body exists but not that I exist, ergo I am not my body"[23]. It can be deduced from Descartes' words that since death is normally thought of as the end of human beings' bodily lives and not the end of lives of the "selves," then the fact that bodies die does not entail that their "selves" die too. The "self" which is also known as the "I" is immortal and eternal, and so can live as a non-bodily being.

Similarly, Swinburne has correctly observed that "it is coherent to suppose that a human being can exist without a body in disembodied form."[24] In simplified form, the argument in behalf of Swinburne's analysis of the "self" and the "I" (belief on life in disembodied body) proceeds along these lines:

(1) If P can be without Q (where P is the "I" and "Q" is the body), then P and Q are distinct.
(2) P can be without Q.
Therefore
(3) P is not Q.

A critical question, however, arises: Is Swinburne's argument cogent? To this question, I agree. It is arguably true that we often naturally talk as if our real selves are distinct from our bodies as when we agree that we can be the same human beings over a number of years despite mereological changes in our bodily constitution. The talk about "the distinction between mind and body and our access to many thoughts such as imagination and thinking without displaying the fact by any bodily behaviour also demonstrates that we are distinct from our bodies[25]. It is curious, however, to note that Swinburne's argument as is Descartes' above, is inadequate. While both successfully proved that our bodies are distinct from ourselves, they did not proceed to demonstrate that life after bodily death is a reality. And, we can only do so by inference.

Consequently, it can be argued that Descartes' and Swinburne's arguments miss the point if we are to use them to epistemologically answer the question on validity and reality of the belief under consideration. Both Descartes and Swinburne can be charged for assuming that if it is logically possible for someone to be without body; disembodied that is, then, one can actually be disembodied, which could be otherwise. This is to say that Descartes' and Swinburne's arguments only prove the logical separation of body and mind. To this effect, Norman Malcom correctly observed that "if it were valid to argue that 'I can doubt that my body exists but not that I exists ergo I am not my body,' it would be equally valid to argue that 'I can doubt that there exists a being whose essential nature is to think'"[26]. Thus, the form of the argument Descartes and Swinburne employ to help establish the doctrine sum res cogitans could be used, if it were valid, to refute that very doctrine; a challenge that might leave the two dumbfounded. It should be noted, however, that though Descartes and Swinburne fail to conclusively demonstrate that there is life after bodily death, at least they help in spelling out that life after bodily death in disembodied form is possible. Their assumptions and contributions are greatly appreciated. They have, indeed, provoked African scholars (like the researcher of this work) to look into the African traditional culture for "elements" which can help to epistemically reconstruct and enrich the belief in life bodily death in disembodied form.

Having made a critique on the failures of some western philosophers in epistemologically prove the reality of the crucial belief of life in disembodied body, we consider African epistemology. The African traditional culture is often overlooked by western scholars yet it is one such "rich culture" which can provide an answer to the problem of life after bodily death which troubles us today. Traditionalists in the African traditional culture claim that they have metaphysical and epistemological powers to communicate with their ancestors (vadzimu in Shona) or departed forebears, in the spiritual world. John Mbiti and S.J Bourdillon refer to the vadzimu as "the living dead"[27] and "ancestor spirits"[28] respectively. Both correctly observe that there is more to human beings in the African world view than the physical body we see. They admit that vadzimu are still living in spite of the fact that their bodies were buried and decomposed. This contention possibly springs from the understanding of personhood by the Africans. As mentioned earlier in this book, Africans define a person by reference to the environing community which comprises both the living and the "living dead".

The "living dead" remains an integral part of the community and can still influence the activities of the community directly or otherwise. Death of the body in the African traditional culture, therefore, is just a transition from this physical world to the spiritual world where "persons" would live eternally in non-bodily form.

The view that there is life after bodily death in non-bodily form in African traditional cultures is further stressed by the holding of ritual ceremonies such bringing the departed spirit back home (kurova guva in Shona) and the appeasement of the avenging spirit (ngozi), among others. According to the kurova guva ceremony, the Shona traditionalists for example, as with most traditional Bantu people believe that when "a human being dies the spirit leaves the body and continues in an afterlife defined primarily in terms of the believed influence of the deceased on the community one has left"[29]. Immediately after death, the spirit of the deceased is considered to be wondering about, unpredictable and potentially dangerous. It can return from the grave to trouble those left behind in the homestead. So, a year or more after the funeral (though the period differs from one culture to another), the kurova guva ceremony is held to calm and settle the spirit among the ancestral spirit guardians of the family, a ceremony which in practice involves pouring libation and condoling the bereaved with quantities of millet beer. If the ceremony is not properly held, the departed spirit may continue troubling the family members and would not protect them in accordance with their physical welfare. In the African traditional culture, this can be empirically/epistemologically checked since communication between the living and the "living dead" can be made possible through the spirit mediums (masvikiro in Shona). After the proper holding of the ceremony, the spirit is now believed to be friendly and can confirm this through "mediums". It can bring fortunes and protect members of the family from all kinds of troubles. This is to say the "living dead" is capable of executing actions.

The metaphysical notion of ngozi in the African traditional cultures can also be used to epistemologically confirm the possibility of life after bodily death in disembodied form. Father Emmanuel Ribeiro, in his novel Muchadura (You shall confess), explains that the avenging spirit can wreak havoc, for example, can cause a series of inexplicable deaths, diseases and unaccountable misfortunes on the murderer and his or her family. In addition to Ribeiro's story, there are many real stories of ngozi (whose effects can be traced and witnessed by anyone) throughout African traditional cultures. The point has to be made here that only living things can execute actions. The spirit of the murdered human being, thus, is capable of causing unfathomable sorrow on the murderer and the family because unlike the murdered body, it is still living and can act accordingly. Those in the physical world can even communicate with the avenging spirit but through spirit mediums or through diviners. When the avenging spirit is appeased it stops its "works" in the family of the murderer. Hence, the ability by the avenging spirit to execute actions and to communicate with those in the physical world shows that life after bodily death in disembodied form is a metaphysical reality and not a myth.

Thus, if we proceed with these investigations, one would observe that there is life after bodily death but in non-bodily form and not otherwise. And, this belief though metaphysical can be proven epistemically using African epistemology as seen above. To allege that there is no life after bodily death in disembodied form as science holds would be therefore a gross misunderstanding, a total failure to understand wholly the metaphysical and epistemological nature of human beings.

There is, of course, much more to be said about the nexus between African epistemology and African metaphysics. No doubt critics will charge that the proposed African indigenous epistemology and metaphysics can never be accepted as legitimate tapestries of knowledge. I doubt this. But I concede that there is more – much more – to be said about the true nature of African epistemology as with African metaphysics. I will turn on to the African Indigenous epistemologies in the next chapter.

Notes

1. Bakari, .S.R. "Epistemology from an Afrocentric Perspective: Enhancing Black Students' Consciousness through an Afrocentric Way of Knowing," University of Nebraska – Lincoln, 1997.
2. Gonese, C. 1999. "The three worlds," in: Compas Newsletter No.1; February 1999 edition.
3. See (http://www.sedac.ciesin.columbia.edu website).
4. Altieri, M.A. Agroecology: The Science of Sustainable Agriculture. 2nd Edition. London: IT Publications, 1995, pp.114.
5.Ocholla, D. 2007. Marginalized Knowledge: An Agenda for Indigenous Knowledge Development and Integration with Other Forms of Knowledge. International Review of Information Ethics, 7(09), 1-10.pp.2.
6. Altieri, M.A. 1995. Op. cit. pp.114.
7. Winch, P. "Understanding a primitive society" in B. Wilson (Ed.), Rationality, Oxford: Basil Blackwell, 1970, pp.79.
8. Mawere. M. 2011.Witchcraft and Possibilities for Cultivating African Indigenous Knowledge Systems: Lessons from Selected Cases in Zimbabwe," Journal of Gender and Peace Development Vol. 1(3) pp. 091-100.
9. Beck, U. Risk society: Towards a new modernity. London: Sage, 1992.
10. Harding, S. (1994). Is science multicultural: Challenges, resources, opportunities, uncertainties? Configurations 2.2, 301-330.
11. See Ikuenobe, P. 2000. Internationalism and the Rationality of African Metaphysical Beliefs, African Philosophy, 13(2), 125-142.
12. Davies, S., McCallie, E., Simonsson, E., Lehr, J.L & Duensing, S. 2009, Discussing dialogue: perspectives on the value of science dialogue events that do not inform policy. Public Understanding of Science, 18 (3).pp.340.
13. Martin Heidegger, The question concerning technology and other essays. New York: Harper and Row Publishers. 1977, pp.4.
14. O'Connor. D.J. (Ed), A Critical History of Western Africa, Free Press, New York, 1985, pp.52.
15. O'Connor. D.J. (Ed). Ibid. pp.52.
16. See O'Connor. D.J. (Ed) .Ibid. pp.53
17. Pearsall. J. (Ed), The New Oxford Dictionary of English, Oxford University Press, 1999, pp.473.

18. Bourdillon. S.J., "Traditional Religion in Shona Society" in Christianity South of the Zambezi, Mambo Press, Gweru, 1973, pp.11.
19. Edwards P. (Ed), The Encyclopedia of Philosophy, Vol. 3 and 4, Macmillan Ltd, New York, 1996,p.38
20. Rouse, W. H. D. (trans), Great Dialogues of Plato, New American Library, New York, 1956, pp.473
21. Rouse, W. H. D. (Trans) Ibid. pp.449.
22. Rouse, W. H. D. (Trans) Ibid. pp.449
23. Descartes, R. "Meditations on first Philosophy" in A Companion of Philosophy, Cambridge Press, 1986, pp.312.
24. Brian Davies. An Introduction to the Philosophy of Religion, Oxford University Press, New York, 1984, pp..218.
25 Brian Davies. Ibid. pp. 218.
26. Brian Davies. Ibid. pp. 218.
27. Mbiti, John S. African Religions and Philosophy, 2d ed. Oxford: Heinemann, 1990.
28. Bourdillon. S.J., Op. cit. pp.11.
29. Bourdillon. S.J., Op. cit. pp.11.

Chapter Five

African Indigenous Epistemologies

The title of this chapter is a bit misleading. The chapter focuses on African indigenous knowledge (AIK) or rather African epistemology, yet it would start with a brief analysis of the concepts of epistemology and knowledge. As mentioned earlier in this book, concepts refer to certain properties, objects or facts in the world. We turn now to the aforementioned concepts in the next few paragraphs.

Etymologically, epistemology is an English concept adopted from Plato's (c. 429-347 B.C.E) episteme which is a Greek word derived from a Greek verb epistasthai which means to know how to (do something) or to be capable of[1] (doing something). Epistemology attempts to distinguish true knowledge from true opinion or belief. Drawing on this understanding, epistemology has been considered as a branch of philosophy which deals with the extent, nature and source of human knowledge; hence the need to examine the concept knowledge.

The question on what knowledge really entails dates back to Plato. In his Theaetetus, Plato defines knowledge as a true belief with an account, in which case an account is justification of what is claimed to be true. Recently, philosophers like A J. Ayers, John Hospers, and Jack S. Crumley 11, among others have come up with a Trinitarian characterization of knowledge as justified true belief (JTB). As epistemologists are much interested in propositional knowledge (knowledge that something is the case) other than knowledge as "acquaintance" and "know-how," knowing in the philosophical sense outlined in Plato's traditional analysis of knowledge requires that for one to be said to know what s/he claims should be true and justified. From Plato's definition of knowledge, John Hospers sets three requirements for knowing a proposition namely: objective requirement, subjective requirement and evidence requirement[2]. These requirements represent the three elements in the tripartite definition of knowledge above, that is, truth, belief and evidence/justification respectively. The requirements set by Hospers stress that for one to claim knowledge of some sort: 1) the claim

77

should be true-truth condition; 2) the agent should believe what s/he claims to be true-belief condition, and 3) the agent should have evidence or justification for what s/he claims to be true. To put it in form of an argument: For a person/subject "A" to know that "P," where P is some proposition, it is both necessary and sufficient that:

1). A knows that P is the case
2). A must believe that P
3). A must have evidence to believe that P.

For epistemologists (both western and African epistemologists), if one fails to satisfy any of the above conditions, then, his/her knowledge claim is void. In fact the subject cannot be said to have knowledge of what s/he claims unless the aforementioned conditions are all satisfied. These conditions are all critical since knowledge in epistemological sense is a result of critical evaluative process not mere coincidence. No wonder Morton had it that: "Knowledge is never a matter of accident or guesswork or fantasy; it must be part of the nature of the process that it gives true belief".[3]

Generally speaking, African indigenous epistemologists like western epistemologists are concerned with identifying the conditions under which an agent can be said to know. In fact they are also extremely concerned with showing that they have knowledge (IKSs) of what they are claiming to be true – JTB. Put differently, all epistemologists are concerned with satisfying the traditional definition of knowledge as true belief with an account/justification; providing the methodological tools that can take us to the truth not falsity.

As can be inferred from the above, the motivation of epistemologists is to defend the claim that we really have knowledge or justification for our beliefs. In many cases, scepticism (a school that doubts about whether we have any knowledge or whether it is possible for us to acquire any knowledge) provokes much of the epistemological debates (debates on African epistemology included). Since the time of Sextus Empiricus, the foremost exponent of Pyhrronean scepticism (a 2nd/3rd century school of scepticism that denied the possibility of people having any knowledge whatsoever) scepticism has always been a threat to our knowledge claims. Epistemologists from all walks of life have since been challenged to defend knowledge claims in their respective areas; hence this book is also a response to the sceptics, particularly those against the existence and legitimacy of African indigenous epistemology systems (AIESs).

There are various versions of IKSs in Africa, but all of them fundamentally emphasize the close connections between the empirical world and the cosmos. This is connection is premised by the belief that empirical world and the cosmos inspire people to have knowledge of many things. Parallels, thus, can be drawn between the consequences of good and bad, given that the cosmological world (nyikadzimu in Shona comprise the ancestors and God/ the creator) govern the empirical world, and in consequence, judges humanity according to the virtue of their deeds. It should be remembered that in African traditional societies, metaphysics and epistemology are difficult to deal with separately as there seem to be a thin dividing line between them. Also, both have always played a central role in perpetuating and easing human life. We shall use the word African epistemology interchangeably with IKS.

In Africa IKSs just like metaphysics were for a long time used to perpetuate a moral, virtuous and knowledgeable society, among other reasons. Though demonized (together with metaphysics) by science and have been labelled superstitious, IKSs remained multifunctional depending on the demands and needs of each society. These systems can still be employed for the very reasons even today. This is what Meki Nzewi urges when he remarks:

> Contemporary Africans must strive to rescue, resuscitate and advance our original intellectual legacy or the onslaught of externally manipulated forces of mental and cultural dissociation now rampaging Africa will obliterate our original intellect and lore of life[4].

What Nzewi advocates here is critical to Africa and to Africans in so far as what is distinctively African in epistemology, morality as in metaphysics in Africa's traditional societies today derive from

African traditional thought and needs. Nzewi reinforces this argument through Touma:

If our ancestors had no sound intellectual mettle, how did they develop the scientific cultures of food, childbirth and mental nurture, also the musical arts genres that were non-sanctionable mediators in the indigenous societal polity and social-cultural practices, including the policing of egalitarian law and order, medical arts delivery, etc.? [5]

To the Africans in general the concept of IKSs is therefore central not only to their metaphysics, but to their moral realm other spheres of life.

It has been argued in chapter four that the providence of science in explaining phenomena owes itself to its internal logic, perceived objectivity and power of prediction that may not immediately apply to African IKSs such as ngozi (avenging spirits), rukwa (fencing property using charm), runyoka (fencing a wife/husband with charm) and zvierwa (taboos). The belief in IKS such as ngozi, rukwa, runyoka and zvierwa is internalist in orientation-it invokes some internally coherent claims about explanation of the functioning of the cosmology to which scientific investigation is less privileged to infer from or draw on[6]. The functioning of these IKSs thus defies recourse to scientific explanation, or prediction to sufficiently substantiate their existence and more importantly practical relevance. Yet the challenge is that the authority of science and its hegemonic influence on epistemology and knowledge production has undermined possibilities for other epistemological alternatives for explicating social reality/nature in ways that fall outside the frameworks of science – particularly how IKSs can illuminate our knowledge of cosmology and what new insights about indigenous knowledge systems could be gained from exploration of this reality.

In this light, I shall argue that "the dominance of science and perceptions about its opaqueness to the public have led to a focus on 'back-end' consequences such as risk, in effect protecting the broader trajectory of scientific and technological development from accountability"[7]. This raises critical questions – questions raised earlier in this book – about whether different forms of knowledge cannot be developed outside the terms and parameters defined by expert science. This will take us back a little bit to the question raised in chapter four: "What is lost in the process of moving from conventional scientific inquiry towards the unorthodox processes of searching for other forms of knowing like examining witchcraft?" I argue that this question cannot be adequately addressed without challenging the monopoly of science as the predominant way of accessing, communicating and transmitting knowledge. The rise in "citizen science" participatory processes of public understanding and even challenging of science research is the direct consequence of public frustration with the limitations of science. In light of this it can be argued, therefore, that IKSs such as ngozi, rukwa, runyoka and zvierwa constitute indigenous knowledge systems that could contribute easing the tapestry of Africa's human development. These IKSs embody a hidden genre of epistemology that could contribute in multiple ways to resolving Africa's development dilemmas, if it cast in the open for debate, and integrated into mainstream expert science. For this reason, these IKSs merit serious discussion. I will now turn on to a detailed discussion of the IKSs, ngozi, rukwa, runyoka and zvierwa. The discussion is meant to determine the possibility of exploring these IKSs as a potentially productive indigenous knowledge system that for long has been conceived as diabolic by Western civilisation and whose developmental essence remains shrouded in mystery.

Taboos as African Epistemology System

Generally speaking, taboos are inviolable/avoidance rules or codes of conduct/commandments used to guide a people of a particular society. These are normally enshrouded in mysteries and indigenous Knowledge systems.

The tradition of taboos has been commonplace in many African societies since time immemorial. While taboos varied from one society to another the purposes of observing them were generally the same. They saved as indigenous values/knowledge systems (IKSs) and belief systems that helped in preserving the natural environment, peace, order, stability and the integrity of African societal structures. However, in many African societies taboos are disappearing, yet with serious social consequences. In Africa, social consequences brought about by shunning these IKSs have manifested themselves in various forms including the rise in crime rates, inexplicable deaths, misfortunes, incurable diseases, moral decadence, ecosystem/environmental degradation and extinction of some wildlife and ecosystems.

The subject of taboos has been approached variably by different scholars. Bozongwana[8] approaches the study of taboos (in Ndebele culture) from a religious perspective. He considers taboos as part of the Ndebele religion, but he groups the taboos according to different people they affect. He noted that there are taboos that affect only children or women or men and others that are general. His categorization of taboos is slightly different from that adopted earlier by Gelfand and later by Tatira. Gelfand grouped taboos into six categories according to themes, namely, "those that talk about living in the correct way, successful pregnancy, avoidance of danger, good behaviour, healthy living, and those conveying religious teachings"[9]. In their analyses both Gelfand and Tatira agree that each taboo had two parts, namely, a "surface meaning" (a lie) and the "deeper meaning" (truth) making some consequences (of violating the taboos) believed by everyone and others believed only by the targeted group (for example children). Concurring with African conception of taboos, Meade argues that in both advanced societies and what he pejoratively calls "savage society": "the motive sentiment is the same, namely, that the things must not be done"[10]. Meade makes it clear that to respect a taboo was an obligation towards society; because whoever broke it caught the taboo contagion and transmitted it to everyone and everything he came into contact with. This implies that taboos behoved the community to enjoin respect for sacred things, and even more, the individual to avoid unnecessary contact with the things enshrouded in taboos.

As noted earlier in this section, although some IKSs like taboos still prevail in Africa, most of these systems have failed to stand the test of time. Others are gravitating towards extinction. This has been due to western scientism and modernity-western hegemonic tendencies that have demonized African IKSs and advanced the view that they were diabolic, barbaric and backward. Nevertheless, taboos which are also known as "the inviolable" or "the sacred"[11] which have been a common tradition in most African societies for centuries now remain a legitimate system of the everyday lives of traditionalists and custodians of the African cultures even today. Taboos include both "real taboos" and "false taboos"[12]. False taboos are those which are only meant to keep check on children. These taboos are only particular to children and not universal as adults know that they are not real – they are empty threats to help control child behaviour. Usagara munzira unozoita mamota (do not sit in the path/road: you will suffer from boils) and usagara pamutanda uri mumoto, unozouraya mukadzi (do not sit on a burning log: you will kill your wife) are typical examples of false taboos practiced among African cultures. The latter taboo, for example, was designed to scare young boys from sitting on burning logs, lest they would burn their buttocks. These taboos are false because their violation does not result in the said consequences. On the other hand, real taboos are those which when violated by any person, young or old, the offender/violator and his/her family suffered serious consequences. It is this tenant that makes taboos qualify as IKSs or rather as a hidden genre of epistemology. As discussed in chapter four and earlier in this chapter, knowledge deals with the nature, source and extent/justification of that which is claimed to be true. Since 'real' taboos are not meant to cast fear in children or anyone using empty threats, but their social consequences are known, then they qualify as IKS. Instances of taboos such as usarara nemusikana/mukadzi ari kutevera kana kuti arikumwedzi unorwara (do not have sex with a menstruating woman as this may result in the illness of the male partner); usatuka, kurova kana kuuraya amai vako, unotanda botso (do not scold, beat or kill your mother as this would result in you suffering from botso, an avenging spirit of your own mother/societal denial if the mother is still alive) and usauraya, unoita ngozi (do not kill other human beings, or you will suffer from avenging spirits) are cases in point. I will return to the latter IKS in a moment. Let me quickly emphasize that the aforementioned real taboos are forms of knowledge in so far as they are justified true beliefs. They pass the traditional analysis of knowledge as JTB. In most, if not all African societies, violations of these taboos bring real social consequences to the culprit and his/her entire family. It is unfortunate that the African elders and scholars though know the epistemological implications of violating the aforementioned taboos could not explain the causal relationships between the real taboos and their consequences which is largely metaphysical and not scientific in nature. I argue that it is this failure to offer an epistemological account of these causal relationships between taboos and their effects on violators/perpetrators that led to the demonization and undermining of taboos and consequently their daunting to banishment in the face of expert science/scientism. Yet, it remains a truism that violation of any of the real taboos in African culture results in fatal ramifications to the perpetrator (and sometimes with his/her entire family). Violation of the real taboo, do not have sex with a menstruating woman as this may result in the illness of the male partner, for instance, would result in the perpetrator contracting sexually transmitted diseases (STDs).

In the light of arguments raised above, it can be concluded that taboos are "codes of conduct/commandments," just like the Biblical commandments and the Hippocratic Oath that guide Christians and physicians respectively, but enshrouded in African IKSs. They (taboos) are commandments/codes of conduct used by the Africans especially before the advent of the Bible with its commandments. Drawing on this understanding, it can be argued that taboos especially the "real taboos" in African societies should be reinstituted as IKSs that help establishing a virtuous, moral society- a society characterized with peaceful, environmentally and morally responsible and caring members. Taboos indeed impact positively on people's behaviour and in peace building processes in many African societies characterized with political and social instabilities like Somalia, DRC, Rwanda, Sudan and Zimbabwe among others. Taboos thus constitute an African IKS /technology (body of ethno-scientific knowledge) that can be equated to the western bodies of knowledge.

The Metaphysics and Epistemology of Ngozi

In the previous section, ngozi has been discussed (though briefly) and justified as IKS. I will now discuss it in some detail in this section.

Technically, ngozi is the spirit of a person who has been murdered by another and then comes back to seek revenge in the family of the murderer by causing unfathomable sorrow through illnesses, misfortunes or a series of deaths until the perpetrator pays reparations to the offended family[13]. It is the avenging spirit called by different names (depending on the language of the ethnic group, for example, it is called ngozi and xipoko by the Shona and Shangana of Zimbabwe and Mozambique, respectively) but premised on the idea of "teat for tat" or "an eye for an eye".

Traditionally, in African cultures, when the guilty family has failed, deliberately or otherwise, to pay restitution (through rites and rituals), it is widely known that ngozi strikes viciously and harshly by not only targeting the perpetrator of the crime but his kinsmen as well. Since Africans believe in the immortality of the soul, it is believed the ngozi knows who killed its body and all the family members of the perpetrator. It is not only the widely known consequences brought about by the ngozi and the rituals and rites involved that make it qualify as a form of IKS, but the fact that it passes the traditional definition of knowledge as a JTB. The truth and justification of ngozi as a belief are represented clearly by the consequences it causes on the perpetrator and his/her family. It is therefore this epistemic quality that makes ngozi an IKS.

As Bourdillon aptly remarks; "ngozi is fearsome and terrifying because it attacks suddenly and very harshly"[14]. It is important to cautiously note that, among the Shona people, for example, it is not always the case that the wrongdoer is the one who gets killed or cursed by ngozi but any person who is a blood relative of the wrongdoer is subject to the anger of ngozi. Ngozi will only stop causing harm and death in the family of the murderer/perpetrator after it is appeased. Otherwise the entire family of the perpetrator together with their properties (i.e. goats, herds of cattle, money and other riches) will all be destroyed. Normally, the victim of murder needs to be replaced by compensation in the form of a herd of cattle and a virgin girl if the murdered person was a man and a herd of cattle and a small boy if the murdered person was a woman. The guilty family thus is given the option to either pay reparations or suffers the consequences through wreaking havoc, for example, causing a series of misfortunes, deaths and illnesses. In a recent interview with the standard Vimbai Chivaura, a Professor at the University of Zimbabwe, acknowledges the reality of ngozi. He comments:

> Haven't you heard people say, usatiparire ngozi? Ngozi imhosva inoda kuripwa (Ngozi is a crime that demands restitution). Prime ngozi arise when innocent blood is shed. If you kill a person you will have terminated all the plans for that person. Even if no one knows that you have done so, you have to acknowledge the crime and pay reparations. When human beings die, their souls would be separated from their body. That soul will torment those who committed crimes[15].

As is revealed in his comment, and indeed so, restitution is part and parcel of the African justice system. Usually life lost is replenished with life; that is why a young girl/boy is usually given to the offended family (the former is normally given in marriage) so as to continue the life of the deceased through her/his off-spring. In the case of the latter, he will have to change his family identity, that is, his surname and the children he will bear will belong to the murdered. This way the cosmological balance disturbed by the outrageous act of murder is restored. This is so because the Africans (especially sub-Saharans) are essentially a spiritual people in general outlook. Their conception of justice is very different from the westerners'. To them ngozi is an integral part of their justice system; it is a form of IKS that essentially expresses disapproval when it comes to actions that result in taking away life; hence to the sub-Saharan Africans ngozi (manslaughter understood in terms of the dire circumstances that follow failure to atone) has a regulatory function epistemically known- that of deterrence rather than retribution.

Due to these atrocities caused by ngozi, the threat posed by the latter is feared by everyone in the African cultures. It is this fear that for a long time has maintained harmony among the Africans and has made them peace-loving people. In view of this observation, I contend that the African societies should continue employing their indigenous knowledge of ngozi to deter potential murderers in their societies. This would lead to the establishment of a virtuous, moral society – a society with people who respect others' rights to life. This paces with values of modern human right teachings at global level.

Metaphysical Epistemologies Enshrouded in Runyoka and Rukwa

Runyoka and rukwa are certainly tied very close together. Given that two allegedly forms of IKSs are closely related, we will discuss them under one section though separately.

The issue of runyoka also known as "fidelity charm" is marred with controversies to the extent that pinning down a precise definition of the concept is not any easy thing. According to International Conference on AIDS, "about 30% of the traditional healers interviewed said runyoka and AIDS were similar, while 68% claimed they could provide treatment for runyoka. Most of the healers regarded runyoka as a weapon used to punish people who committed adultery, while some said it was a way of determining whether a wife/husband was faithful"[16]. According to the same report, a few said it was a method used by some people to punish enemies through their wives. Almost all the traditional healers interviewed claimed medical doctors could not cure runyoka because it involved witchcraft and required a herbalistic or traditional approach. Healers also felt that medical doctors should take traditional healers seriously and give them a chance to look at AIDS patients.

Since violation of runyoka results in a mysterious disease, I define runyoka as a complex venereal disease caused by sleeping with a fenced (using herbs/charm) woman/man. The fencing can be done by either partner to ensure that the spouse would not be involved in prostitution or adulterous activities. In a report given in Herald (of Zimbabwe), Seremwa, a native of Gambura village, Chinhoyi recently died in mysterious circumstances after complaining of severe stomach pains and later acting like a fish before spending two nights in a bathtub filled with water. She would intermittently gulp the water and then spew it out like a fish. Hospital medical superintendent Dr Collett Mawire confirmed the strange incident. A woman who saw Seremwa when she was at the hospital said:

> Seremwa was complaining of suffering from extreme heat and dehydration whenever she got out of the water and had confessed to being intimate with a man who had been "fixed/fenced" by his wife. The practice is known as runyoka or "fencing" in many circles. Seremwa further that the man's mother had warned her not to hang around with the man indicating that he had been fixed with runyoka by his wife. She regretted not listening to the man's mother[17].

In another incident, Doktorsnake website told that the Mount Darwin secretary for the Zimbabwe National Traditional Healers' Association, Benson Kaseke, said of runyoka:

> Although runyoka is not approved by traditional healers, it is widespread in the Mukumbura area of Mount Darwin, on the border of Mozambique. Runyoka is typically used by people who suspect their spouses of playing away from home as no one wants to live with an unfaithful partner, hence the need for runyoka[18].

Kaseke further explains that in some cases daughters are given runyoka by their parents so that they cannot engage in premarital sex.

As can be seen, runyoka is a "safety lock" applied on both men and women to enforce fidelity. The fact that the practice is enshrouded in mystery and is linked to witchcraft as it may result to death of the perpetrator, has made expert science to demonize and campaign for its banishment in African societies. It can, however, be argued that such distortions and misconceptions arise from the pollution of traditional African culture by colonialism and expert science. It remains a reality that runyoka enforces fidelity between spouses and can therefore be used to establish a highly moral society which might also be free from sexually transmitted diseases such as HIV/AIDS pandemic. The shunning away of the practice by many African societies seems to have expedited the rate at which Africans are contracting STDs like HIV/AIDS. Cases of rape, adultery and premarital sexual relationships are also on the rife; a reality that could have been otherwise had it been that runyoka is being used in all societies. It is my contention therefore that if IKSs such as runyoka are continually used in Africa societies and beyond, this would help to establish a morally virtuous society – a society that might be free from STDs and c rimes to do with adultery and rape.

Of the same genre in African metaphysical epistemology is rukwa (fencing property with charm). Though a common practice among the Shona people of Zimbabwe and Mozambique as well as the Chewa of Malawi, especially in the countryside, there is scarce recorded literature on rukwa[19]. Among the Shona themselves, the Ndau people (an ethnic group under the umbrella Shona) are most well-known for the use of rukwa in safeguarding/protecting their property from thieves and invaders. It is in this light that we define rukwa as medicine/charm used to safeguard or fence property from thieves and invaders.

In an interview I held in Manica Province of central Mozambique, the Ndau traditional healer, Sekuru Gogoyo revealed that:

Rukwa is used to safeguard one's property by mysteriously catching the thief and prevent him/her from escaping until the owner arrives. One of the most common methods of administering rukwa are the use of a small bottle. One would secretly put some traditional herbs (given by a traditional healer) in the small bottle, closes the bottle and dumps it at the doorstep of his/her bedroom, shop or field (where s/he wants to protect the property). The magic charm would catch any thief that dares coming to steal away the property[20].

The rukwa charm thus safeguards and prevents the property in the house, shop, field or any other place where the property is kept. Any thief or invader that dares coming in to steal away the property risks the humiliation of being caught in the act by the owner, as s/he supposedly would be unable to leave the premise because of the power of the magic charm. "The thief can only be freed when the owner comes, summons the community to witness the event and then strikes the thief two to three times using a whip,"[21] added Sekuru Gogoyo. As can be seen, rukwa is multifunctional as it does not only protect property from thieves, but brings the thief to shame.

Though some people due to western influences link rukwa to witchcraft, I argue that to understand the logic of rukwa fully one has to seek its meaning and relevance in the culture where it is a being used. In fact, rukwa as with runyoka is a "safety lock" applied by some Africans on thieves to enforce in them good behaviour or respect of other people's property. Rukwa turns thieves into fully responsible citizens by deterring them from tampering or stealing away other people's property. In the light of this understanding I contend that the IKS, rukwa should be continually used in African societies and even beyond if a morally virtuous society is to be established. In fact, rukwa though an epistemological genre enshrouded in African metaphysics continues a better security guard and, a good "moral teacher" for thieves.

Witchcraft as Indigenous Metaphysical Epistemology

The discussion on rukwa and runyoka in the previous paragraphs leads us to a discussion on a controversial IKS in African metaphysical epistemology – the notion of witchcraft (uroyi/uloyi in Shona and Shangana, respectively). From an African view point, witchcraft is the spiritual skill of being able to carry out certain inimical activities in disembodied form, but sometimes in bodily form. This could include sucking of blood, eating, holding of meetings, causing accidents or inflicting pain or diseases. In Africa, there abound many proven cases of the activity of witches and wizards – those involved in witchcraft activities. This shows us that African experience surpasses the narrow causal epistemological framework of western philosophy. The scientific model is therefore not absolute. There is the method of extra sensory perception (ESP) which can be used by those so endowed to understand the more complicated causal framework in which African experience fits. Witchcraft is a real phenomenon; hence it passes as metaphysical epistemology framework. The study of spiritism, occultism, mysticism, and cybernetics reveal that man is a carrier of great current of waves which can be projected to bring about certain desired ends however, with some limitations.

That said, I should be quick to remark that the heated debate on what constitutes witchcraft has been futile because it has been riddled by confusion activated by dearth of precision in definition of terminology and the context driven nature of witchcraft. This complexity of developing a precise definition is implied in Bowie[22] who analyses witchcraft through the lenses of taxonomy than a concise definition: She provides the following classification of witchcraft:

1). Malefice: medieval European practice of cursing or healing, and the manipulation of people or objects.
2). "Adversaries of Christianity and agents of Satan".
3). African witchcraft: associated with the ethnographic works of the Anthropologist Evans-Pritchard on witchcraft and magic among the Azande.
4). The rise of modern era metaphysical beliefs in western culture which has seen the rise in neo-pagan witchcraft including Wicca.

While this classification is illuminating in terms of identifying the contextual origin and the different forms that witchcraft often takes, it is less informative with regards the definition of witchcraft. Further, although the classification provides some insights into medicinal or pernicious properties of witchcraft, its connections to the metaphysical realm particularly God and Satan (celestial beings that operate in cosmology that are immune to scientific verification) - the evil or the underworld- it leaves us perturbed by what the practice of witchcraft is, and what are the finite aspects of its anatomy.

Similar definitional limitations are observed on the Zimbabwe's Witchcraft Suppression Act (ZWSA) conceptions of witchcraft. The ZWSA (Chapter 73) defines witchcraft as "the throwing of bones, the use of charms and other means or devices adopted in the practice of sorcery"[23]. This broad definition is unyielding and futile as it leaves a lot to be desired. It confuses witchcraft with sorcery, and throwing of bones is not necessarily done to identify or drive out witches, as many judiciary officials and lawyers now realize. Rather, the throwing of bones is a means of divination, that is to say, a means by which a diviner or traditional healer determines, or attempts to determine who or what caused an illness, death or other misfortune complained of by an individual or a group. Thus the ZWSA and Bowie's conceptions of witchcraft are too conflated and misleading, and therefore philosophically implausible.

A common notion underlying witchcraft is the metaphysical belief that supernatural forces may be used as a means to achieve certain complicated indigenous knowledges/epistemologies and personal goals which include harm, profit and fertility. In this view, I shall define witchcraft as a practice that involves the use of potentially harmful medicines, charms, magic and any other supernatural means or devices to cause some positive effects (such as wealth accumulation, social power) or negative consequences (such as psychological or physical harm, illness, misfortune or death of other people, animals or property). This is because witchcraft beliefs embrace a wide range of ideas, practices, and motivations, but in their various forms they usually share the idea that the power to inflict injury and benefit could be exercised through unobservable, supernatural means[24]. Witches and wizards – those involved in the practice of witchcraft – are thought to possess extraordinary powers that enable them to perform ritual practices and act beyond the capabilities of ordinary human beings. They are deemed capable of travelling great distances at night using winnowing baskets or of having the ability to turn themselves into hyenas, or of going out in spirit and killing a victim while their bodies remain at home in bed[25]. As such, beliefs in witchcraft are often used to explain fortunes and misfortunes, good and evil, life and death. These negative connotations about the practice instil fear into humanity and foreclose possibilities for unpacking the productive potential of the practice. However, the negative connotations attached to witchcraft do not take away the justification of witchcraft as a metaphysical epistemology or rather as a form of IKS.

Though enshrouded in mystery and with negative connotations, it can be acknowledged that there are a number of epistemological, medicinal and social benefits witchcraft practice could accrue to society if the practice is considered an ethno-science (indigenous knowledge) and is "tamed". This can be achieved through a process of "de-robbing" the practice (witchcraft) from its "diabolic garment" by exploring and incarnating from it those elements that are negative –doing away with the negative connotations that witchcraft possesses- and leave with it only those elements that are positive. We shall call this process "witch taming". I propose, in the next few paragraphs we focus on why and how witchcraft practice can be exploited as an IKS with development potential, and that can complement science especially in providing explanations to issues of metaphysical epistemological nature. Expert science cannot provide explanations to such issues as they are outside the canonical frameworks of scientific inquiry

The failure of science to explain other phenomena raises critical questions about whether different forms of knowledge cannot be developed outside the terms and parameters defined by expert science. What is lost in the process of moving from conventional scientific inquiry towards the unorthodox processes of searching for other forms of knowing like examining witchcraft? This question cannot be adequately addressed without challenging the monopoly of science as the predominant way of accessing, communicating and transmitting knowledge. The rise in "citizen science" participatory processes of public understanding – and even challenging of scientific research is the direct result of public frustration with the limitations of science. This chapter can not necessarily be conceived as a chapter on citizen science, but rather as one that seeks to argue that witchcraft constitutes an IKS that could contribute easing the tapestry of Africa's human development. That is to say, it can be argued that witchcraft embodies a hidden genre of epistemology that could contribute in multiple ways to resolving Africa's development dilemmas, if it is cast in the open for debate, and integrated into mainstream expert science. As such, I further my argument that the exploration of witchcraft (especially in Africa where the practice is rampant) as IKS can be a potentially productive exercise. To substantiate this position, we turn, therefore to suggestions on how and why witchcraft practice can be exploited as an IKS with development potential that could benefit the public.

Witchcraft has a dualistic quality of being good or bad, positive or negative and it is its positive quality that is "abused," yet can be exploited for the common good once the practice is "tamed" and fully recognized as an IKS, per se. Many Africans, through their personal experiences, acknowledge the existence of witchcraft as an indigenous knowledge system (IKS). Surprisingly, most of the African governments due to the colonial influences in their statutory laws are still adamant or rather ashamed to fully recognize witchcraft as a form of IKS. I argue, this is fallacious reasoning being committed by African governments given that in one way or another, they all believe in the existence of both the physical and spiritual worlds. In fact, by acknowledging that there is the physical world and the spiritual world one is acknowledging the possibilities of beings in the metaphysical world whose metaphysical powers might harm or bring fortunes. And if an IKS is a body of knowledge or bodies of knowledge of the indigenous people of particular geographical areas that they have survived on for a very long time[26] and that can be passed (secretly or otherwise) on to another through rituals or rites, then, witchcraft qualifies as one form of IKSs. Unfortunately, none of the believers in witchcraft have conquered their fears enough to negotiate with the witches to adopt their ethno-science for public good. In Africa, witchcraft ethno-science remains a hidden secret and none has strived to tap from its productive potential. As such, it remains an "abused" and "lost" science whose essence regrettably, has been "unexploited" for common good.

In light of this observation, I argue that African governments, and by extension the global world, should fully recognize the practice and find possible mechanisms of engaging with the witches in order to understand their indigenously developed "scientific knowledge" or "ethno-science" to benefit the majority. In fact African governments should realize that the differences that exist between witches and traditional healers are just semantic, yet traditional healers' work is legalized and witchcraft is illegal. Given that witchcraft can be appropriated for both good (wealth acquisition, generate bumper harvests) and bad, the negative application of witchcraft (abuse) is most likely a culmination of constraints in conceptualization on the appropriate, effective use of magical powers embodied in indigenous knowledge. As such, if witchcraft is recognized by the African states governments and its positive benefits underscored while its catastrophic effects are abolished, its positive permutations can be affirmed.

Taking it further, western science is a holy grail across the world because it has been acquired, distilled and documented in ways that are readily usable (readable, allowing for sustainable use by the posterity), transmittable and patented. On the contrary, the reason why witchcraft as an "ethno-science" has not been a productive indigenous knowledge is because it has been shrouded in mystery, not transparently transferable and has been given strong pejorative connotations. If IKSs are to be developed, then local beliefs and value systems about the functioning of the cosmology like witchcraft should be given credence in this quest.

Realizing this, some African governments are beginning to take bold steps towards full recognition of IKSs in general, though still ashamed to fully recognize witchcraft as another form of IKS. Commenting on the South African government's adoption of an Indigenous Knowledge Systems Policy in South Africa, Lesley Green emphasizes that the motivation for such an extensive commitment to the idea of indigenous knowledge from government is underpinned by the desire to restore dignity to African knowledge; to de-racialize the ways in which African knowledge has been collected, archived, and used, and in relation to international debates around indigenous knowledge and its legal protection[27]. I infer from Green that the need to restore dignity in African knowledge and de-racialize African indigenous knowledge production is premised on the realization that much of the knowledge production processes about Africa, and for Africa have been externally executed, with many possibilities for misrepresentation, misinformation about Africa by foreign writers. All this constitutes underutilization and misappropriation of African knowledge systems and witchcraft is one such practice from which rich indigenous knowledge can be documented by Africans for Africans and the world. Witchcraft constitutes vast, untapped knowledge or ethno-science whose productive potential remains unsubstantiated and underestimated owing to its opaque form and mystery. If witchcraft is captured and appropriated, a process I have already named "witch taming," this "abused," and "lost" indigenous knowledge could be used in manifold ways to support Africa's human development agenda.

Contributing on how witchcraft can be exploited, I invoke Adam[28] who cogently observes that vital information on health, child rearing, natural resource management is often encoded in unique forms such as proverbs, myths, rituals, and ceremonies but often shunned for modern scientific techniques and thoughts. Witchcraft is one such indigenous knowledge base that health professionals, traditional healers and policy planners can draw on, integrate it with other scientifically generated information to enrich or to indigenously manufacture curative medicine, herbs and healing practices. Herbs from witchcraft practices can be purified and patented as medicines and integrated in mainstream health education programmes that benefit African nations and the world at large. Alternatively, witchcraft as an IKS can become an alternative form of knowledge system that complements the mainstream scientific knowledge systems. Given the contested nature of scientific discoveries, the term "citizen science"[29] has been coined to describe independent investigations that the public conduct to understand contentious issues on science or issues science has failed to provide convincing explanations to the public. The examination of the medicinal properties of witchcraft could be a launch pad for effecting "citizen science" aimed at liberating Africans from over-dependence on modern science for production of expensive drugs. A useful health information database can be developed from witchcraft confessions that target extraction of health information, transmission and preservation. Given the perspectives and claims raised by indigenous people's groups whose emphasis is usually on the autonomy of local tradition of knowledge and ways of life from modernizing states and development paths, substantial gains can be acquired from developing witchcraft as a form of alternative IKS.

Also, the beliefs in witchcraft are often strongly tied to the struggle over resources, relations of production and configurations of power. Rich people (particularly successful farmers) who dwell in impoverished communities are often accused of bewitching others and of having a form of witchcraft called divisi (agricultural charm). Divisi is a charm that helps witches and wizards to acquire wealth particularly bumper harvest and big herds of cattle. As such, Geschiere cites Comaroff and Comaroff who suggest that a close nexus between forces of modernity and witchcraft:

> Witches...embody all the contradictions of the experience of modernity itself, of its inescapable enticements, its self-consuming passions, its discriminatory tactics, its devastating social costs[30].

While this observation evokes the view of the dilemmas that arise from structural tensions between forces of globalization that reinforce a consumerist culture on the one hand, and traditional societies with limited access to goods of ostentation on the other, I seek to extend this structural analysis. Given the fact that some successful farmers, upon interrogation concede to the use of divisi, there are grounds to argue that instead of denialism about its existence, divisi could be explored further to inform indigenous biomedical technology research that could benefit Africa's agricultural potential. While the potential of IKSs to support human development has been acknowledged in Africa, limited concerted strategies have been put in place to draw on it. For example, it is common knowledge that at the height of Zimbabwe's fuel crisis, half-hearted attempts were made by government to manufacture diesel from cactus plant, despite indigenous knowledge's proof that biodiesel was extractible from this plant. By the same token, the agricultural potential of divisi should not be underestimated by Africa and the world at large.

Besides, as is known by many born and raised in Africa, wizards and witches have been accused of causing miscarriages and barrenness among African women, and wizards are accused of committing sexual misconducts with victims' unsuspecting wives without their consent, a practice called mubobobo (in Shona). Notwithstanding its strong ethical flaws (non-consensual sex), the capacity for mubobobo (sexual misconducts with victims' unsuspecting wives without their consent) to promote reproductive health cannot be underestimated. Demystifying this witchcraft practice through promoting public education about the practice, unravelling its secretive foundations and regulating consensual sexual conduct constitute bold steps towards eradicating the high incidences of unprotected sex, sexually-transmitted diseases (for example, HIV/AIDS) and promotion of balanced reproductive health. If need be, ways of integrating this indigenous knowledge into mainstream "expert" reproductive health could be forged. This is premised on the understanding that both IKSs and global systems of knowledge production are informed by some cultural bases, values and attitudes. As Leach and Fairhead[31] aptly suggest, fundamentally, both local knowledge and science should be seen as emerging and developing through historically located practices, in particular institutional and social contexts, subverting any fundamental theoretical divide between them. Mubobobo should not be imposed on unsuspecting women with debilitating effects like miscarriages. Rather possibilities for its integration with established expert knowledge on artificial insemination on wiling infertile women could be envisaged.

I contend that the African practice of turning a blind eye on the metaphysical epistemology of witchcraft and other such IKSs constitutes denialism that works to exacerbate problem of victims falling prey to the negative application of the practice. We can draw some parallels between this kind of denialism to that of former South African President Thabo Mbeki who denied that HIV virus causing Aids, and this had debilitating effects on the population. Recent research shows the regime of Mbeki's failure to roll out HIV drugs between 2000 and 2005 resulted in 330,000 additional deaths and the infection of 3,500 infants with HIV[32]. In the same vein, cynicism about witches and sorcerers, or to eradicate "witchcraft science" without unravelling it may short-change Africa in terms of tapping from this "ethno-science". Africans could succumb to many diseases if positive witchcraft knowledge was explored, would be curable. Considering the billions of dollars that Africa spent on treating patients who are bewitched, critical questions arise: "What could be more efficient to engage witches in developing curative practices integrated with scientific research or footing the lofty health bill spent on curing bewitched patients? How much indigenous knowledge could be derived from unravelling witchcraft practices?"

More so, witches are believed to trigger mheni (indigenously generated power) that can set ablaze victims, their houses, property, and herds of cattle. To define it in a bit of some detail, mheni is believed to be a traditionally developed form of lightning that witches can trigger on victims even on cloud free days. The mheni carries high voltage and travels at exceptionally high velocity but causes death of people, irreparable damage to property or animals. I am convinced that if some ways of capturing mheni for electricity generation and transmission could be developed; the power outages and the incessant blackouts that have robbed Africa of its industrial production potential could put to rest. I believe that as knowledge production becomes transdisciplinary, sociologists and anthropologists should look beyond their disciplines for solutions to the daily problems that haunt society. As such, "no professionals of any discipline should be content with the mere logical consistency of a theory at a given moment in time."[33]

Lastly, but more curious is the fact that although witches are believed to glide for thousands of kilometres in winnowing baskets at night, no one has ever conceptualized the possibilities of applying this traditional science for conventional long distance flights to less navigable areas or support "space exploration" missions. While conventional wisdom could approach this supposition with cynicism, it should be remembered that it was not until some brilliant inventor invented a cell phone that people came to understand that wireless communication through handhelds (mobile devices) was possible. Using the same logic, it can be argued that instead of surrendering to the corridors of scepticism fellow academics and researchers should develop unorthodox means of exploring this new field of enterprise (space exploration using the winnowing basket).

Underscoring the arguments raised in this section, I submit that the discourse on the indigenous knowledge and scientific research potential on witchcraft should transcend disciplines and invoke the commitment of scientists, traditional healers, philosophers, social anthropologists, and the witches themselves as collaborative working groups. Limited ground breaking research on witchcraft, particularly in the area of its positive human development potential has been achieved as researchers are bent on drawing lines between scientific research and social science research. Yet, it has to be remembered that "drawing a boundary at a particular point on a continuum can create paradoxes; it can lead to polarization of knowledge, mirror identifications, and endless repetitions of mistaken views."[34] In light of this, I argue for collaborative research across disciplines on witchcraft in ways that allow for integration of knowledge and development of new insights on the subject; hence calling for more discussion on witchcraft by scholars from across disciplines.

Notes

1. Tiles, M. (Ed), An Introduction to Historical Epistemology, Blackwell Publishers: Oxford, 1993, pp.11.
2. Jacques P. Thiroux, Philosophy, Theory and Practice, Macmillan: London, 1985, pp.488.
3. Morton, P.K. (Ed), A Guide Through the Theory of Knowledge, Cambridge University Press, 1977.
4. Nzewi, M. A Contemporary Study of Musical Arts: Informed by African Indigenous Knowledge Systems. Volume Four Illuminations, Reflection and Explorations. Ciima Series, 2007, pp.4.
5. Ibid, pp.7.
6. Mawere, M. 2010. Indigenous Knowledge Systems' (IKSs) Potential for Establishing a Moral, Virtuous Society: Lessons from Selected IKSs in Zimbabwe and Mozambique, Journal of Sustainable Development in Africa,12 (7) 209-221.
7. Davies, S., McCallie, E., Simonsson, E., Lehr, J.L & Duensing, S. 2009. "Discussing dialogue: perspectives on the value of science

dialogue events that do not inform policy". Public Understanding of Science, 18 (3), pp. 340.
8. Bozongwana, W. Ndebele Religion and Customs. Gweru: Mambo Press, 1983.
9. Gelfand, M, The Spiritual Beliefs of the Shona: A Study based on fieldwork among the East-Central Shona, Gweru, Mambo Press,1982, pp. 138.
10. Meade, H.M.T. The Origin and Universality of Taboo and Totemism, Harare: Native Affairs Department Annual, 1930, pp.17
11. Pearsall, J. The New Oxford Dictionary of English. New York: Oxford University Press, , 1999, pp.112.
12. Mawere M and Kadenge M 2010, 13 Zvierwa as African Indigenous Knowledge System: Epistemological and Ethical Implications of Selected Shona Taboos, INDILA -Journal of Africa Indigenous Knowledge. Vol.9. (1) pp.13.
13. Mawere, M. "Life After Bodily Death: Myth or Reality?" in Zambezia Journal of Humanities, University of Zimbabwe: Harare, 2005, pp.11.
14. Bourdillon, M.F.C. The Shona Peoples: An Ethnography of the contemporary Shona, with Special reference to their Religion, Gweru, Mambo Press, 1976.
15. Standard Newspaper, 23/05/2010. Ngozi: primitive superstition or reality?, http://www.thestandard.co.zw (accessed 12 May 2010).
16. International Conference on ADIS, 1993. http://gateway.nih.gov/ (accessed 2 June 2010).
17. Herald 20/03/10, http://thenational.newspaperdirect.com
18. DoktorSnake, Africa: Land of magic and sorcery, on April 30th, 2010, http://en.wikipedia.org/wiki/Africa (accessed 2 May 2010).
19. Mawere, M. Indigenous Knowledge Systems" (IKSs) Potential for Establishing a Moral, Virtuous Society: Lessons from Selected IKSs in Zimbabwe and Mozambique, Unpublished, 2010.
20. Interview with Sekuru Gogoyo, Traditional Healer, Manica Province, Mozambique, (20/04/2010),
21. Ibid
22. Bowie, F. The Anthropology of Religion—An Introduction. Blackwell Publishing, 2006.
23. Tredgold, J. Witchcraft Suppression Act, 1943. Chap. 46.pp.194.

24. I ascribe to the view that the difference between positive witchcraft (witchdoctors, or traditional healers) and negative witchcraft (witchcraft, sorcery) is semantic and academic. I argue that negative and positive witchcraft are different in the most unimportant respects. Both apply supernatural powers, involve the use of charm or magic, are connected the cosmological world and most importantly can be employed to do both good and harm depending on the motivation of the individual involved (healers or witch).
See also Mutungi, O.K. The Legal Aspects of Witchcraft in East Africa with Particular Reference to Kenya. Nairobi: East African Literature Bureau, 1977. pp p.xviii.
25. Middleton, J. and. Winter, E.H. Witchcraft and Sorcery in East Africa, London: Routledge & Kegan Paul, 1963.
26. Mapara, J. 2009, Indigenous Knowledge Systems in Zimbabwe: Juxtaposing Postcolonial Theory. The Journal of Pan African Studies, 3(1), pp.140.
27. Green, L. 2008, Anthropologies of knowledge and South Africa's Indigenous Knowledge Systems Policy' Anthropology Southern Africa. 2008, 31 (I &2), 48-57.
28. Adam, L, 2010, Information and Communication Technologies, Knowledge Management and Indigenous Knowledge: Implications to Livelihood of Communities in Ethiopia [Access at: www.eictda.gov.et/.../Knowledge_Management_and_Indigenous_Knowledge.doc Date accessed: 2010/02/16].
29. Irwin, A. & Wynne, B., (Eds) Misunderstanding Science? The Public Reconstruction of Science and Technology. Cambridge: Cambridge University Press, 1996.
30. Geschiere, P. 1998, Globalization and the Power of Indeterminate Meaning: Witchcraft and Spirit Cults in Africa and East Asia. Development and Change, 29, pp. p. xxix.
31. Leach, M. & Fairhead, J. Manners of contestation: "citizen science" and "indigenous knowledge" in West Africa and the Caribbean, UNESCO, 2002, pp. 299-311.
32. Nattrass, N. 2009, Gender and Access to Antiretroviral Treatment in South Africa. Feminist Economics, 14 (4), 19-36.

33. Chavunduka, G.L. 1980, Witchcraft and the Law in Zimbabwe, Zambezia, Journal of Humanities, University of Zimbabwe, V111, pp.144.
34. Holland, I.R. Self and Social Context. London: Macmillan, 1977, pp. 272.

Chapter Six

African Indigenous Ways of Knowing

African indigenous ways of knowing are many. If recognized, they can be used as complementary modes to reinforce the legitimacy of the already known sources of knowledge like sense experience, reason, authority, tradition and common sense, among others. As such, this chapter identifies 'indigenous' ways of knowing traditionally used by Africans and argues for their recognition as legitimate sources of knowledge, besides those that science offers.

Categorizing African Ways of Knowing

African epistemology is already equipped to discuss 'indigenous' ways of knowing – knowledge systems produced through 'indigenous' thinking or exploration whether material, philosophical or linguistic. This is because it contains four basic ways of knowing: divination, revelation, intuition, and reason which can be separated into the categories of supernatural, natural, and paranormal. In addition, African epistemology has humans' relationship to the supernatural as one of its fundamental Afro-centric themes of transcendent discourse along with human relations and human relations to their own being[1]. Thus, a synthesis of knowledge, spirit, and cosmos is acknowledged in African epistemology. This being the case, the cultural practices of the African people and their descendants should be recognized as valid sources of knowledge with the same legitimacy as Western epistemology.

Senegalese scholar Cheikh Anta Diop commenting on the advances of western knowledge observes, "man is a metaphysical being and it would be catastrophic if a genetic or chemical manipulation were to take away his innate anxiety"[2]. For Diop and indeed so, this anxiety is man reconciling himself with himself and to bypass this process using scientific knowledge means would make him cease being himself, a "being" with a destiny, no matter how tragic. This statement, by one of modern Africa's most prolific and renowned scholars underscores the importance of acknowledging, integrating, and balancing metaphysical and physical knowledge and "being". It stresses that scientific or rather epistemological knowledge without a metaphysical basis and reflection is void; it leaves some invisible metaphysical gaps and, hence is insufficient. This justifies the legitimacy of African ways of knowing that attempt (though at a level that can be considered by expert scientists as elementary) to encompass all the three aspects, metaphysics, science and psychology. Depending on the degree to which they interact with these three aspects, African ways of knowing vary. Yet embedded in all these cultural ways are technologies that have distinct epistemologies which have implications beyond ritual and tradition. In the next section, I discuss the ways of knowing common to Africa.

The Supernatural Way of Knowing

In African cosmology, the supernatural is considered a way of knowing the unknown through mystical means. However, the said is twofold and so has two variations namely divination and revelation. For purposes of clarity, I shall look at the two variations separately.

Divination

The word divination derived from the Latin noun divinatio-onis f. divino which means "the gift of prophecy, divination," formed from the past participle of the verb divinare, "to foretell, prophesy, forebode, divine the future". This noun is closely related to the adjective divinus-a-um, "belonging or relating to a deity, divine"[3]. Cicero, in his treatise De Divinatione (Concerning Divination) informs us that the Latin word, because of its derivation from divinus, meaning belonging or relating to a deity, was an improvement on the original Greek word mantike, derived from mania (furor in Latin), which meant madness, raving, insanity, or inspiration[4]. Considering these two definitions, divination can be understood as a way of exploring the unknown in order to elicit answers to questions beyond the range of ordinary human understanding. It should be quickly noted that divination always involves complementary modes of cognition associated with primary process and secondary process of thinking or knowing. This tantamount to saying diviners are specialists who use the idea of moving from a boundless to a bounded realm of existence in their practice. This movement makes diviners to excel in insight, imagination, fluency in language and knowledge of cultural traditions. During divination process, they (diviners) construct usable knowledge from oracular messages. To do so, they link diverse domains of representational information and symbolism with emotional or presentational experience.

Divination has had a critical role in the classical world, especially in ancient Egypt and the Middle East, the Americas, India, Tibet, Mongolia, Japan, China, Korea and Africa[5]. Subjects of divinatory inquiry are many. They include complex questions about past events, the present and the future, disasters (past and present) whose causes cannot be explained, things hidden from sight or removed in space, proper conduct in critical situations like healing of illness and diseases, religious worships and making choices of persons for particular tasks[6]. Giving the cases of the Shona and Yoruba (as with many other African cultures) diagnosis of illness (àrùn), it would, for example, include divination to be sure that any potential spiritual causes are identified so they can be addressed in the treatment[7]. Among the Dagara, methods of healing always take into account the energetic or spiritual condition that is in turmoil, thereby affecting the physical condition. This is because focusing just on the physical is considered as denying the needs of energy, the adjustment of Spirit needed to make the cure last[8]. This energy finds a new and more potent way of impacting the body, thus by addressing the energy of the mind and Spirit, whose status is affecting the physical body, then, you are likely to heal truly. Thus generally speaking, African cultures involve divination in one way or another whenever confronted with serious problems like illness or inexplicable diseases and deaths.

Perhaps one more important thing to note is that there are many ways of divination in Africa. These include water and crystal gazing/vibrations, casting of lots or sortilege, dreaming, the reading of natural omens, the taking of hallucinogenic drugs, contemplation of mystic spirals, amulets, abyrinths, mandalas and thangkas[9]. Most of these ways of divinations are a common feature in many countries in southern Africa like South Africa, Zimbabwe, Mozambique, Malawi and Zambia. Although I enjoy explanations and philosophical debates over each of these ways of divination, we will not delve into further details. I will only emphasize that in all the afore-stated ways, the diviner undergoes either physical or psychological changes (depending on the way of divination) so as to be able to serve as a vehicle for divinatory powers. In some instances, animals, objects and events themselves are considered signs of external superhuman powers that can bring solutions to the problems in question.

Revelation and Faith

Revelation and faith are allegedly two separate ways of knowing that are certainly tied very close together. For this reason, we will discuss them together.

Revelation is a form of supernatural knowledge that involves one being aware of the unknown (which s/he could not have discovered through any other sources) via dreams or visions from a deity or some sort of supernatural source. To gain and recognize this as true knowledge, one should have faith (a strong belief) in the revelation. African traditionalists like religious people in general, consider faith as a source of knowledge for two major reasons: 1) Faith makes supernatural knowledge possible to them and, 2) they (African traditionalists) believe that if they have faith that certain propositions are true, they will be, and the faithful will then have special knowledge they wouldn't otherwise. Knowledge of medicinal plants is a practical example. This is often received in dreams from animals or some sort of supernatural source. In one legend, a Blackfoot woman with tuberculosis noticed beaver tracks and left food for the animal, which returned the favour by appearing in her dreams to give her a cure for her illness. She tried the remedy – an infusion of lodge pole pine resin – while singing. After much vomiting, her chest cleared and she became well[10]. This type of herbal knowledge received during dreams was not accepted unthinkingly but was subjected to empirical tests of its effectiveness.

Revelation, though is normally private and unobservable to others for verification as can be seen in the above example, it can also be public. There are many examples of public revelations in Koran and the Bible.

What makes revelation and faith valued ways of knowing in Africa is that in African cosmology, spirit is found conceptually and etymologically in all categories of being and even though an entity is a "thing per se" it still has a life force. This life force is the power, force vitale, or energy that resides in all creation. Its qualities are such that it is found in varying levels of intensity in the universe at different times. It is traditionally believed among African traditionalists that the energy that resides in all creation – force vitale – allows a person to interact with the supernatural world during revelation thereby receiving knowledge of the metaphysical epistemology constructs or of the unknown through revelation.

The Natural Way

Intuition is another source of knowledge often claimed by some philosophers and religious people (African traditionalists or otherwise) and, can "mean many things to different people, from hunches/feelings and wild guesses, to mystical insights, to a higher form of reason"[11]. In general, intuition means direct apprehension of truth or a kind of quick, direct, or immediate perception of knowledge and insight. I should be quick, however, to mention that the idea of intuition as conceived by Africans is something in need of elaboration. Offhand it may not sit very well in the minds of those unaccustomed to the view of intuition presented in this book. Generally speaking, African epistemologists understand intuition as a natural feeling or sign in one's body that enable one to be aware of certain facts, truths or events. They see intuition as immediate knowledge, immediate awareness, rather than as a rational process like reasoning or logic. Self-awareness, self-consciousness, abstract thought and the ability to understand relationships (naturally or somehow effortlessly) in logic, mathematics, between thoughts, ideas, feelings and propositions are all forms of intuition. In African traditional cultures, all these forms of intuition are considered above and beyond the regular type of reasoning (as rationalists give) and sense experience (as empiricists give). For this reason, intuition seems difficult to distinguish from internal sense experience – one's own inner states/inner life. Giving an example of knowledge attained through intuition, particularly hunches or feelings: "One may say I had a feeling that it will rain". The implication of this statement is that there is some sort of special kind of knowledge available (at least to the person himself/herself) through the way s/he feels or through some other inexplicable means. The reliability of such knowledge would depend on how often "intuitions" – hunches or feelings – paid off to the extent that people who had them were right about any claim they had made from this source. I am reminded of my grandmother when I was growing up. We used to call her a prophet of weather. Whenever she woke up feeling her right leg aching she knew a day would not pass before rain start pouring. The same was true with her right eye's upper lid. Once it strikes incessantly she knew the day would not pass before receiving good news. The opposite would occur with her right eye's lower lid, she used say. Though her knowledge of what would happen in the near future was private to her and could not be fully verified by expert science, it was valid as it always produced positive results. To consider her knowledge a guess work or fantasy would be wrong. Her knowledge claims can pass the traditional analysis of knowledge as justified true belief.

Note, the understanding of intuition explicated above is not very far from the Western understanding of intuition as "the direct apprehension of truth: the immediate knowledge about a fact, or truth, as a whole and the awareness of past, present, or future events without the conscious use of such processes as linear reasoning, rationality, or analytics"[12]. African epistemologists like Western epistemologists agree that intuition enables an individual to have insight into a situation without having all the details or facts. They also believe intuitive knowing is a universal human experience and a key element in discovery, holistic problem-solving, understanding, and knowledge generation. It may be described as "gut feeling" or "sixth sense"[13] in so far as intuition can be experienced as a spiritual connection between the person and the environment or between persons-in interpersonal connections.

Paranormal

African paranormal is demonstrated in proverbs, idiomatic expressions, riddles, and other critical literary genres. Riddles, for example, are an important logical tool in the traditional African system of education. Riddles are "puzzles or word play"[14]. This definition shows that riddles involve two main aspects namely, reasoning, particularly inductive reasoning skills, as implied by puzzles and recreation as indicated by play. While African riddles have important functions like socialization and recreation, they also played the fundamental role of sharpening one's reasoning skills and quickness of wit, as well as fostering quick mental flexibility on the part of the child as he/she grapples with different possibilities and probabilities in the search for correct answers to given riddles. The process of solving riddles, for example, involves logical inference and the justification for answers based on reasoned analysis of the posed riddle. African riddles, thus, apprentices reasoning skills and ideas that enable a person to comprehend and explicate reality. It is for this reason than that riddles can pass as a form of indigenous knowledge.

As has been seen with riddles, proverbs are a critical genre in African epistemology. Indigenous proverbs can be understood as creative expressions, using the local language, symbols and reasoning processes used to translate a text (signification), value and meaning. They are often short, pithy statements that are easy to remember. As such, they are symbols or signposts of oral cultures (like African traditional culture) in so far as they help one from an oral culture to understand primal religion, local culture and facilitate development projects. Walter Ong resounds this understanding when he emphasizes that oral cultures rely upon formulaic expressions and mnemonic patterns in order for people to remember what was said[15]. This connotes that proverbs are particularly useful (as sources and preservers of indigenous knowledge) in oral cultures. Giving an example of development projects, proverbs can facilitate these by providing a comprehensive basis for African social structures and indigenous logic to determine how the former can be successfully implemented.

Underscoring the epistemological value of proverbs in Africa, John Mbiti lamented its lack of study. He observed: "Proverbs are common ways of expressing religious ideas and feelings. It is in proverbs that we find the remnants of the oldest forms of African religious and philosophical wisdoms"[16]. Researching on Akan culture, James Nkansah-Obrempong affirmed this observation. He aptly noted: "In these [Akan] proverbs, therefore, one can see the wisdom and soul of the Akan people"[17]. Ghanaian philosopher and author, Kwame Gyekye, [18] exemplifies how Akan proverbs can be analysed in order to highlight the meaning and extract the African values embedded within. He grouped the proverbs and analysed their content in order to give a broad understanding of the African worldview. Gyekye also utilized proverbs in order to construct a moral philosophy of the Akan people. In doing so, he attempted to describe a general African worldview and philosophy.

Yet, while Africans have placed great epistemological value on their proverbs, unfortunately, this was not widely shared by Westerners in the past. Nussbaum observed: "In some extreme cases such as Liberia and Swaziland, missionaries took such a negative view that to this day there is a virtual taboo on the use of any proverb in Christian preaching."[19] It is only in recent times that Western scholars and missionaries have begun to appreciate the value of proverbs as the bases of African wisdom and knowledge. A five-day international conference – Proverbs and African Christianity Conference – was held in Mozambique in March, 1995 to discuss African proverbs and their connection to Christianity and religion in Africa. And, the consultation entitled, "Embracing the Baobab: The African Proverb in the 21st Century" was held in South Africa in October of the same year, 1995 for the same purpose of promoting and raising the profile of African proverbs. For example, in the CD, Joyce Penfield notes: "African proverbs are the sacred texts of African Traditional Religion and thus are a paradigm for understanding sacred tradition."[20] This claim indicates how the study of proverbs can be critical to understanding primal religion. The proceedings from both are recorded on a CD ROM.16.

Besides, both conferences are believed to have increased the networking of historians, theologians, missionaries, philosophers, sociologists, social anthropologists and cultural researchers in African epistemology research. It contains over 25,000 proverbs from at least 27 different languages, along with bibliographies, and research studies. Following the two African proverbs projects mentioned above, regional centres were initiated in South African, Ghana, Kenya, and Cote d'Ivoire for data collection and research promotion. A web site (www.afriprov.org) now is also devoted to African proverbs, stories, and sayings that includes daily proverbs along with a "Proverb of the month" that provides an explanation of the meaning and biblical application.

On Behalf of African Metaphysical Epistemology

Truth is certainly one of the hardest things to come by. Worse still African metaphysical epistemological truth! It is hard enough to resolve rationally and through the principles of expert of science, the metaphysical and epistemological questions addressed in the preceding discussion. One would even think it best not to seriously consider questions of African metaphysical epistemology. To this kind of thinking, I feel obliged to re-echo my principal argument in this book that 'indigenous' epistemological and metaphysical questions are not everyone's taste. What, however, remains a truism is that metaphysical curiosity and quest for understanding 'indigenous' epistemologies are a worthy and even sometimes a noble human characteristic. This is what David Hume meant when he correctly observed: "It is almost impossible for the mind of man to rest, like those of beasts, in that narrow circle of objects, which are the subject of daily conservation and action"[21]. When we venture of such a narrow circle, we unavoidably bump into questions of metaphysical and epistemological natures. Actually, human beings can hardly eschew having some representation of themselves, other human beings and the world. This representation is the beginning of metaphysical and epistemological reasoning.

It is my conviction that the preceding discussion might not take us far toward a deep and comprehensive understanding of African metaphysical epistemology. However, I remain hopeful that enough has been said, at least, to help reconstructing and pronouncing African epistemology and African metaphysics as disciplines worth studying in universities and colleges.

More importantly is my fervent hope that enough has been said to encourage readers to take stock of their favoured view of the world and to seriously consider the possibility that the representation I made in this book may, in some respects, be in need of revision. I hope, too, that no metaphysician or epistemologist will seriously entertain the hypothesis that there are as many worlds as there are representations of it and that there are therefore no uniquely correct answers regarding questions of metaphysical and epistemological natures. I believe what may differ are the approaches to the subjects and not the truth beneath.

It goes without saying that mistakes are common. No doubt, my position in this book may contain mistakes and my own representation of the African world and the world in general is in a distressing number of ways incomplete and of course in many ways in transition and possible process of protection. I invite the reader to bring this to light. However, some of my metaphysical and epistemological beliefs paraded in this book seem to me both well-founded and unlikely to require revision.

Finally, I say that African metaphysics and African epistemology are a hodgepodge of beliefs and realities which are the outcome of African lived experiences. Appearance is not wholly reality to the African as it to the Westerners. The physically perceptual level holds a different kind of reality while the spiritually perceptible holds quite another level. Both are regarded as real in a sense but in cases of conflict, the African will hold to such truths or realities that have been corroborated and confirmed by spiritual means. At some level, the Africans may adopt seeing as believing attitude while at other times they insist on consummate verification before they can believe. It appears that all things are first taken to be real until proved otherwise. All in all, we have cursorily examined the different dimensions and aspects of African metaphysical epistemology but I want to add that these views are not static. In fact, today hybrid metaphysics and epistemology is fast becoming the order with African traditional metaphysical epistemology merging with Christianity, Islam, Eastern religions and Western conceptions of reality.

Though this work is far from saying all that needs to be said, it only intends to ignite more discussions on the idea of African metaphysical epistemology and African philosophy in general; to call for the reversal of the Eurocentric paradigms of Africa where the perjured interpretations of Africa have remained grafted on the mental processes and human aspirations of most modern Africans thereby robbing them of their intellectual confidence and mental identity with regard to posterity. This thrust can make more sense if universities recognize the strengths of African metaphysical epistemology, and embrace it as a means to foster a positive environment for African people inside and outside the continent. This would ensure that imperialism, though has intimidated, would fail to conquer the African consciousness. It is my fervent hope, in the words of Nzewi, therefore that:

> After the bombardment of the invading tornados of fanciful knowledge, the Indigenous lore of life will yet revive with innately refurbished shoots, and fulfil again the human mission of the musical arts in original Africa, and edify Africa's mental and human posterity[22].

It is this similar hope encapsulated in most African scholars that binds Africans and, will help redefine Africa. No wonder why Asante had it that "the negative images of Africa will not remain forever locked in the negative chambers of the past [but] an Africa that is freed of the imposition of others and consequently an Africa that could rise at any occasion"[23].

Notes

1. Asante, Molefi Kete. The Afrocentric Idea, Philadelphia: Temple University Press, 1987, pp.168.

2. Diop, Cheikh Anta. Civilization or Barbarism: An Authentic Anthropology. Eds. H.J. Salemson and M. de Jager. Translated by Yaa-Lengi Meema Ngemi. Chicago: Lawrence Hill, 1991, pp.366.
3. Cassell's Latin-English/English-Latin Dictionary, 1955.
4. Pease, A. S. (Concerning Divination, Vol. 2, Urbana, 1920-1923, (reprint Darmstadt, 1963, pp. 12-13.
5. Loewe, Michael and Blacker, Carmen (Eds) Oracles and Divination. Boulder: Shambhala. 1981.
6. Barbara Tedlock, Divination as a Way of Knowing: Embodiment, Visualization, Narrative, and Interpretation, Folklore Society, 2001.
7. Ambiola, W, Ifa Divination Poetry, New York, 1977, pp.30.
8. Somé, Malidoma Patrice. The Healing Wisdom of Africa: Finding Life Purpose Through Nature, Ritual, and Community. New York, NY: Jeremy P. Tarcher/Penguin, 1997, pp.30.
9. Pruce, J. Divination Systems: Ways of Knowing, Bloomington: Indiana University Press, 1991.
10. Lipp, F. J, Herbalism: Healing and Harmony Symbolism, Ritual, and Folklore Traditions of East and West. Boston: Little Brown, 1996, pp.105.
11. Jacques. P. Thiroux, Philosophy, Theory and Practice, Macmillan: London, 1985, pp.480.
12. Rew, L. & Barrow, E. 1987. Intuition: A neglected hallmark of nursing knowledge. Advances in Nursing Science, 10 (1), 49-62.).
13. Benner, P. (1984). From novice to expert: Excellence and power in clinical nursing practice. Menlo Park, CA: Addison Wesley, 1994.
14. Chesina, C, Oral Literature of the Kalenjin, Nairobi: East African Educational Publishers, 1994, pp.14.
15. Walter J. Ong, Orality and Literacy (London, UK: Routledge, 1982; reprint, 1989.
16. John S. Mbiti, African Religions and Philosophy (Garden City, NY: Anchor Books, 1969; reprint, 1970, pp.86.
17. James Nkansah-Obrempong, "Visual Theology -the Significance of Cultural Symbols, Metaphors, and Proverbs for Theological Creativity in the African Context: A Case Study of the

Akan of Ghana," Journal of African Christian Thought 5, no. 1 (2002), pp. 38.

18. Kwame Gyekye, African Cultural Values, an Introduction (Accra, Ghana: Sankofa Publishing Company, 1996.

19. Nussbaum, (Ed). The Wisdom of African Proverbs Cd Rom, Version 1.03 Introduction, Record 14/78.

20. Joyce Penfield, "The African Proverb: Sacred Text in Praxis, in The Wisdom of African Proverbs Cd Rom, ed. Stan Nussbaum (Colorado Springs, CO: Global Mapping International, 1996), 1024.

21. Hume in Treatise of human nature, Oxford University Press, Oxford, England, 1960: pp.271.

22. Nzewi, MA Contemporary Study of Musical Arts: Informed by African Indigenous Knowledge Systems. Volume Four Illuminations, Reflection and Explorations. Ciima Series, 2007, pp. 5.

23. Asante, K.W. Zimbabwe Dance: Rhythmic Forces, Ancestral Voices-An Aesthetic Analysis, Trenton: African World Press, Inc., 2000, pp.xv.

www.ingramcontent.com/pod-product-compliance
Lightning Source LLC
Chambersburg PA
CBHW020618300426
44113CB00007B/693